Living *the* Empty Nest

A life beyond mothering

DR TERESA O'BRIEN

Copyright © 2025 Dr Teresa O'Brien
ISBN: 978-1-923601-04-8

Published by Vivid Publishing
A division of Fontaine Publishing Group
P.O. Box 948, Fremantle
Western Australia 6959
www.vividpublishing.com.au

NATIONAL
LIBRARY
OF AUSTRALIA
A catalogue record for this
book is available from the
National Library of Australia

To my dear friend, Jenny. I have learned by watching you, listening to you and following your gentle ways. Your friendship taught me many things. And even though life has taken much from you, your beautiful soul remains. You remind me that love lives nearby even when our nests are empty.

Author's Note

This book is based on stories and conversations gathered over many years through personal experience, professional work, informal interviews, and community involvement. Many names and identifying details have been altered to respect privacy and protect identities. Some stories are composites, merging the voices and experiences of multiple women into a single narrative. Others are fictionalised accounts inspired by common themes and recurring truths shared with me.

While this narrative centres on mothers, it warmly acknowledges fathers, single parents, non-traditional families, and diverse caregivers, including LGBTQ+ parents, foster carers, aunties, uncles, and kinship networks. The pain of letting go and questions of identity are not confined to biology or gender. These pages are for you, too, offered in an open-hearted spirit.

Any direct quotes attributed to individuals such as "Fatima" and others are either paraphrased, recreated with permission, or used as illustrative dialogue to reflect broader emotional or cultural experiences. These are not meant to represent any specific person unless explicitly stated. While the details may have been adjusted, the emotional and cultural truths remain. This book is a testament to the real, lived complexity of the empty nest experience across diverse backgrounds, and it is offered with deep respect to all whose stories shaped its pages.

Some chapters in this book reference AI platforms. These are shared as practical examples of how digital literacy is changing, not as contributors to the writing itself. Every word in this book is my own.

Table of Contents

PART IV RECONNECTION AND GROWTH

For the Journey Ahead

Introduction:
The Part No One Prepares You For

I was behind the wheel, driving my twelve-year-old daughter down a national highway, my eyes wet with tears on a face I struggled to dry. Why was I driving away from her when every cell in my body longed to turn the car around and bring her home? Her bedroom still held soft toys and tiny shoes. This wasn't supposed to happen yet.

But out here in rural Western Australia, where the paddocks stretch to the horizon and the next roadside mailbox might be ten kilometres away, boarding school isn't a choice for many families. It's the only option. So one by one, our three daughters packed their bags and left home, not for good but for large stretches of time.

The empty nest didn't arrive when my daughters turned eighteen and left for university. It came in instalments, starting when they'd only just turned twelve.

Years later, I stood in the same driveway, watching the red dust settle behind the car. For a long, painful moment, I realised I had no idea who I was meant to be. The house was still. Our daughters were gone, not just for a term this time, but truly gone. And I was just... here.

The cycle had finally ended, but the grief hadn't. After over a decade of rehearsed goodbyes, of letting go repeatedly, of living in emotional limbo, this final departure felt both familiar and utterly devastating. No one tells you that the empty nest isn't just about missing your children. It's about losing yourself.

Where were the books for this piece of life? The part where your role dissolves, your days lose rhythm, and everything you thought you knew about yourself crumbles away. And especially, where were the books for those of us whose empty nest arrived early, years before we felt ready?

Bookshops overflow with guides for every other transition: pregnancy week by week, sleep training, toddler tantrums. The teenage years fill entire shelves. Financial advisors discuss retirement: the portfolios, the downsizing, the pickleball and pottery classes. There are books for divorce, grief, menopause, and reinvention at fifty.

That's when I knew this book needed to exist.

Maybe it happened gradually for you: shoes lined up by the door, jackets hanging undisturbed on their hooks, and teacups always in the cupboard. The pulse that once beat through every wall, cracked window, and creaking floorboard has ebbed away, leaving only a deep, patient stillness. Either way, you can feel it; the house holding its breath.

This book is for you: the mother whose days once hummed with purpose and now stretch out in ways you never imagined. You're not alone. I've walked this road, felt the crushing loneliness, and somehow found my way back. I don't have all the answers, but I know this: we don't just survive this stage. We can thrive in it. Let's walk this path together.

When the Nest Empties Too Soon

I never imagined this moment. Perhaps I didn't want to face the reality that someday they would step into adulthood and leave. Nothing prepared me. Their bedrooms still held soft toys and tiny shoes. This wasn't the natural course I expected. It was an early form of letting go, arriving years before I felt ready, and filled with heartbreak.

One daughter left without looking back. She adapted well to boarding school life. Another rang home every night during her first year, wanting to be with her family and the animals on the farm. The youngest missed home, too. They still needed nurturing and the sense of safety that home provided. When each daughter's time to leave came, the same sorrow and grief returned reliably as the seasons.

I wasn't ready to stop mothering.

Every new term meant packing another bag, dropping someone off, covering more kilometres between us. Each time they returned, the house briefly filled with colour and noise, only to fall silent again. Every departure felt like ripping off the same old Band-Aid, term after term, year after year. The cycle of rehearsed goodbyes taught us to let go repeatedly. For over a decade, we lived in emotional limbo, constantly releasing, reattaching, and releasing again.

As time moved on, it didn't get any easier. The school bus still passed each morning but no longer stopped. The road stretched long and familiar, with questions I hadn't yet learned to ask. The absence wasn't just a gap in routine; it was a complete reshaping of the everyday. Like many mothers, I told myself this was temporary, a phase, like teething or tantrums. But the tears, the heartache, and the emptiness pressed in, no matter how busy life remained.

Other rural parents I met at boarding school dinners and parent events shared the same stories. One mother called it *the grief that comes in waves you can't outrun*. Another described driving 800 kilometres to see her daughter and get a hug before turning around and driving home again.

The geography might change, but the heartbreak doesn't.

My Story, Our Story

Although this book begins with my story, it is not mine alone. Throughout these pages are the voices of women I've spoken with across Australia and beyond, mothers whose stories echo with struggles, triumphs, and renewals. Their words serve as invitations into a broader conversation that is often overlooked.

You'll find narrative, guidance, companionship, reflections, and advocacy here. Along with personal stories, this book explores cultural narratives, societal silences, and policy gaps, inspiring new ways to support and celebrate women during this transition.

My rural perspective shapes the stories I tell, but the emotions in these pages extend beyond fences and borders. Grief and wonder at an empty nest are universal, no matter where you live. By sharing my story, I hope you'll see parts of your own, even if the landscapes differ.

Throughout these pages, you'll encounter 'she', a narrative voice drawn from my life, shaped by the landscapes, emotions, and moments I've experienced. She is not a universal woman, but a familiar one. She is each of us: past, present, and emerging. These 'she' vignettes start in my world and form part of my story. They are written with the hope that others will recognise something of themselves in her.

You will find a broader perspective here. Although the empty nest is a personal change, it's also a cultural blind spot. By understanding why the empty nest has gone unexamined, you join the movement to break that silence. Reading this book places you within a community of parents reclaiming this stage as a valid, powerful, and transformative part of life.

What This Book Offers

The empty nest is one of life's most common transitions, yet it's also one of the least acknowledged. Unlike birth, adolescence, or menopause, there is no shared language to guide you through it. Parents are told to celebrate their children's independence, but few talk about the grief, disorientation, and identity shifts that happen once the bags are packed.

This book validates what many parents feel but rarely say: that letting go is both an act of love and a source of pain. It provides words for emotions you may have found hard to express, stories that reflect your own, and strategies to help you find balance.

You might arrive at the empty nest happily, even enthusiastically, embracing your newfound freedom with anticipation and openness. Your experience is valid. Others feel the weight of loss deeply. Whatever way you arrive, this book offers companionship, reflection, and encouragement, especially for those in rural and regional areas where support networks can be limited.

In the following chapters, we'll explore the landscape of the empty nest in its many forms. We begin with the emotional terrain of release before moving on to how identity, relationships, and the home are reshaped. Later chapters examine self-care, freedom, friendships, digital life, career and purpose, travel, grandparenting, and legacy.

Some chapters might initially seem unexpected, particularly those on career, digital connection, and travel. However, they are not distractions from the emotional journey but expressions of it. These themes stem from lived experience. Rediscovering purpose, learning new technologies, and saying yes to adventures were lifelines for me. These chapters reflect the modern aspects of the empty nest, especially for women adjusting to a world that continues to move, digitally and socially, around them.

Each chapter ends with reflections and practices, small pauses to step into your own story. There's no right or wrong way to use them. Some may inspire lots of writing or thinking, while others may provide a quiet reflection moment. Both are valuable. View each exercise as an invitation. Choose the most helpful ones and revisit those that resonate with you later.

This is where we begin, in the afternoon of a sunny day. Who were you before, and who might you become now?

PART I:

SEEING, NAMING, AND UNDERSTANDING THE EMPTY NEST

Chapter 1

The Emotional Landscape

She was only twenty when she left the west coast behind and stepped into the vast, open wheatbelt land, a girl in op-shop boots, sporting a punk hairstyle and an attitude that threw caution to the wind. She had fallen for a man who was a farmer.

While her contribution to the farm was immense, she also developed a deep appreciation for work through diverse early roles. She pumped fuel at roadhouses, weighed grain trucks on weighbridges, sold airtime at a radio station, and connected recruiters with job seekers in employment offices.

She was a student. When her children were born, she studied whenever she could, at night and into the small hours, while breastfeeding them, during their sleep times and on weekends when their dad was around. She was a nurturer. She also fed the shearing teams, her family, orphaned lambs, dogs, stray cats, guinea pigs, and birds. She was isolated. She was new to town. Her parents were hours away. Family support was a phone call or a three-hour drive. She was a mother. The children grew, and she raised them for the present, not for the future, loving them, nurturing them, teaching them everything she knew.

Yet, she never imagined how quickly her three daughters would grow up. They were taught to be kind, strong, and independent thinkers, as well as farm helpers, with tasks such as lamb marking, sheep drafting, and rock picking. She packed school lunches, birthday cakes, netball, hockey, and cross-country uniforms. She watched them get on the school bus each morning and the train to boarding school in later years. Each time they left, she cried.

When they finally left for good, one after the other, ready to step out into the world, what was left was even harder to imagine. It was a kind of anguish, unlike ordinary sadness or grief, like childbirth, impossible to grasp until you're in it.

Who was she going to be without them? What was wrong with her? Surely other mothers felt this, too. No one discussed this part: how the house stays tidy but feels cold and empty, how much you miss them. These moments weren't marked. There were no parties, no celebrations for their leaving.

Sorrow and inexplicable grief overwhelmed her. She buried herself in her work, studies, and whatever else she could to distract herself. She still had more than half her life remaining. Over time, a sense of wonder grew. Beneath the purpose of that maternal life, something was waiting for her.

Personal Stories

This chapter explores the journey of the empty nest, from parents' initial emotional reactions when children leave home to the realisation that their lives are only just beginning, filled with many unexpected opportunities. It also offers some strategies to manage these emotions and the realisation that this stage brings.

I spoke to women across towns, cultures, and nations who weren't afraid to share their memories and reflections, many still raw years after their children had left. This may have been their first real chance to express their feelings openly. There are few moments to share such experiences in the natural course of parenting, making these exchanges particularly meaningful. Their stories reveal the struggles and successes of the empty nest phase, offering honest insights and inspiration. A farm woman, used to open spaces, reports that although her house felt very empty, she misses the noise but has learned to enjoy the peace. She described it as a strange feeling, where loneliness and freedom happily coexist. Another woman moved to the city to be with her daughter. She described her daughter's departure as a loss no mother should have to bear. Such diverse emotional responses characterise the emotional nest experience. For many, however, the most vivid memories return to a single turning point when everything began to change.

The Moment Everything Changes

You sense the change before fully understanding it, even before their physical departure. It shows in glimpses of empty seats around the table, quiet Sunday afternoons, and moments of startling silence. The washing machine sounds much louder when it's only half full. Cooking for two instead of five. Car journeys seem to go on forever. Suddenly, you're an empty nester, and the emotional adjustment begins. You realise you've been preparing your children for this moment their whole lives, but no one prepared you.

Some parents notice the impending change months

or even years beforehand, as conversations shift to jobs, university applications, gap year plans, or career aspirations. Anticipating grief can be just as overwhelming as the actual separation, leading to a period of emotional adjustment that catches many by surprise.

Perhaps you might not have the luxury of a gradual preparation. You face a sudden departure, such as a military deployment, an unexpected job opportunity, or a relationship challenge that pulls your child away with little warning. The emotional whiplash can be intense, shifting from active parenting to an empty nest without the psychological buffer zone that anticipatory grief provides.

For parents of only children, the empty nest has a unique finality that families with multiple kids don't experience. There are no practice runs with older siblings, and no remaining children to soften the silence. When the only child leaves, the house changes from a family home in a single day. Helen, whose son left for university, reflected: *I kept thinking, this is it. Other parents get to do this gradually, but it was like a flipped switch for us.* The absence feels more complete, and the identity shifts more firmly. No more school pickup schedules, no other children's friends filling the space, and no younger sibling to focus attention on. This finality can heighten grief, sadness, and eventually the sense of freedom.

You're not imagining all this. According to the Australian Seniors' Empty Nesters Report 2024, which surveyed 1,208 Australians aged 50 and over, the emotional impact of children leaving home is significant.[1] As you might find, the emotional bonds don't just vanish when their physical presence ends; they change and continue long after your children become independent.

But solitude isn't always despair. It's a threshold, and like many new beginnings, it brings both vulnerability and strength. Beneath these immediate emotional reactions lies a deeper question that arises once the initial shock passes: if your children no longer need you in the same daily, hands-on way, who are you now? The psychological turmoil can be intense.

Though this experience is deeply personal, it is far from isolating. This moment is particularly complex for women because it often coincides with other significant midlife changes. Some navigate this phase while caring for ageing parents, dealing with career pressures, and managing physical changes in their bodies. Others face financial restrictions that limit their dreams of travel and reinvention, and some operate within cultural contexts where children traditionally stay at home until marriage, all adding layers to an intricate emotional journey. Their stories challenge the stereotype of the mother who smiles and waves goodbye to her children, revealing the complex reality underneath. The overlapping demands of the empty nest amplify the emotional toll, layering sadness, restlessness, and anxiety.

For some, the first year feels like a free fall. One mother admitted she couldn't enter her daughter's bedroom; the lingering scent of body spray, memories of bedtime chats, and the silence were too overwhelming. Another mother described her sons' departure as feeling like being stabbed in the stomach and torn apart. Others packed away family photos because being out of sight was out of mind.

Such diverse emotional reactions expose a fundamental

truth. There's no "right" way to feel when children leave home. Some women describe feeling as though they're mourning a death, while others feel like they're being reborn. All experiences are valid and thus deserve recognition and support.

When They Don't Need You Every Day

Stepping away from a role that has shaped you for decades feels like parting with a whole identity. It can be overwhelming, stirring feelings of loss, loneliness, and uncertainty, and it does not resolve easily. For some, it appears like a fog. For others, it is a sharp and sudden cut. When the caregiving role diminishes, the grief is not only for the physical absence of children but also for the rhythm of closeness that has disappeared. For today's parents, technology softens but doesn't remove this absence. A FaceTime call, a photo popping up on WhatsApp, or a quick text can make a connection in seconds, emphasising the gap between digital presence and physical closeness.

The emotional impact can feel especially unsteady if you're a single parent. The silence can seem complete without a partner to reconnect with or share the transition. Ashleigh, who raised her daughter alone after a divorce, described the first evening: *I kept waiting for someone else to come home. But it was just me, and I realised I hadn't been 'just me' for eighteen years.*

You might have built your adult life around your children's routines, social needs, and emotional demands. With your children gone, your daily routine shifts. This can make you feel as though you're losing your main source of connection and comfort, increasing your feelings of loneliness and vulnerability.

Maria, a city girl, felt this change profoundly. Her kitchen had been her command centre for twenty years, with homework spread across the bench, permission slips signed amid stirring dinners, and the constant hum of teenage life. The morning after her youngest left, she stood in the spotless kitchen, listening to the neighbour's lawnmower. This familiar, comforting suburban sound had been drowned out by family noise ever since the kids were born. Her house felt cavernous, amplifying every faint sound she had never noticed. The silence in her home was the absence of being needed, a different kind of quiet altogether.

While being on your own again without children offers promise and opportunity, the journey to discover it is rarely straightforward. In fact, many women find themselves blind-sided by emotions they never expected. The woman in the opening vignette experienced feelings far beyond sadness, restlessness, emptiness, longing, and sometimes even unexpected relief.

You might find this passage to be a deeply personal journey. Without cultural scripts or templates to steer you, feelings of purposelessness, disorientation, or grief can surface unexpectedly. Your child's perfume in the bathroom vanity might bring on unanticipated tears. Noticing a favourite cereal brand becomes a small reminder of their absence. These immediate, almost instinctive responses to their absence may catch you off guard with their intensity.

One woman described this first stage as grieving for someone who is still alive but no longer present in daily life, a response which psychologists call 'ambiguous loss'.[2] This type of loss can be particularly disorientating because there are few social markers or support systems to help process it. Such initial reactions, however intense, are just the start of a more complex emotional landscape that often develops over the following months.[3]

Mothers, long shaped by societal expectations of being the primary carers, often feel this more acutely than fathers, carrying the emotional load in ways that aren't always visible. Fathers also undergo a complex emotional shift. Some feel relief from less financial stress or more time with their partner, while others experience emotions they seldom express until asked. One father shared his grief and nostalgia as he walked past his son's unused cricket gear in the shed, realising it marked the end of years spent cheering from the sidelines. Another reflected that, while he welcomed fewer financial pressures, he found the evenings stretched longer than expected. Although cultural expectations can make it harder for men to express this loss, their feelings of pride, emptiness, and adaptation are just as valid as women's experiences.

Contradictory Emotions

Beyond the recognised sadness, many parents face conflicting feelings that clash with their expectations. Relief might be swiftly followed by guilt for feeling relieved. Excitement about newfound freedom can be dampened by anxiety about managing it. Some describe feeling invisible, as if their social identity is so connected to being someone's mum that they struggle to introduce themselves without those familiar labels.

For some women, the strongest emotion isn't sadness at all. It might be relief, excitement, or even joy. *I thought I'd be devastated*, shared Claire, stretching in her pyjamas at 9 am on a Tuesday. *But honestly? I feel so alive, a real sense of freedom. For the first time in twenty years, I can eat what I want, when I want. I can leave dishes in the sink, travel on a whim, and work on who I am when nobody needs me.* Her relief was genuine, and her guilt about that relief just as real. Two truths can exist in the same heart without cancelling each other out.

These mothers may have spent years looking forward to this moment, counting down the days to the freedom they knew was coming. Some describe feeling like they've been released from a wonderful but exhausting prison of constant caregiving. Yet, this celebration can be tinged with guilt. Society expects mothers to be devastated by their children's departure, not to celebrate their own private milestone. The shame around feeling excited, and the worry that joy makes them a "bad mother," can overshadow what should be a time of genuine celebration.

Instead of showing confusion or instability, this emotional complexity mirrors the natural human response to major life changes. The guilt over feeling relieved, the anxiety linked to excitement, and the shame about celebrating independence are not part of the adjustment process.

Knowing that these conflicting emotions are normal and temporary can help parents approach them with more self-compassion, whether grieving the loss or celebrating freedom. As the initial shock subsides, certain feelings become constant companions. These emotions may rise and fall but often reappear in different forms over months or years.

Enduring Emotions

Nostalgia and Reminiscence

Nostalgia often becomes a strong companion. Parents reflect on their children's earlier years, cherishing memories of bedtime stories, school plays, sports events, or shared laughter on family holidays. Sometimes, it lives in objects: the crayon drawings fade on the fridge, the sports clothes still faintly smell of grass, the childhood books sit on the shelf. This heavy sense of nostalgia makes it hard to step into their children's rooms, let alone change them. The door stays shut, not from neglect, but from respect. To disturb the room is to disturb memory itself. To interrupt the memory is to reopen the wound. Few admit that sometimes the wound needs reopening before it can heal.

This intense emotion can prevent women with an empty nest from moving forward. How do you let go of baby clothes still folded in drawers, early school year diaries, and well-loved teddy bears? How do you decide what to keep—every drawing, school report, and treasured toy? Or you don't keep anything. You might want to photograph the items and store them digitally. Nostalgia signals that the love and years invested are still part of you. Accepting your need to hold onto these memories, instead of dismissing this feeling, involves acceptance. Such joyful memories from earlier days can also increase another persistent emotion often linked to this journey: the ongoing worry for your children who have left.

Worry

Worries don't shrink when your children leave; they simply expand to fill the space between you. It's often said that the older your children get, the more you worry about them. A study tracking parents through the empty nest transition found that 80% reported ongoing concern for their adult children's wellbeing, with this anxiety often peaking during the first year after they leave.[4] You raised them to leave, so you need to learn to trust that the foundation you've built will hold without your daily oversight. While it's normal and loving to worry, unchecked anxiety can become overwhelming. Building trust in your children's abilities and shifting your role from parent manager to supporter can help lighten this emotional load.

Pride

Watching children grow into independent, capable, and responsible adults fills a deep sense of pride. For many parents, this marks the culmination of years of emotional investment, practical support, and guidance. There is great satisfaction in seeing the values, skills, and confidence they have fostered take hold and thrive.

Pride becomes an emotional anchor during times of personal upheaval. Parents often find that linking their children's independence to the effort they put into raising them brings a deep sense of satisfaction and even eases the pain of loss. Watching a child navigate their first job, manage their own household, or handle challenges independently affirms that the parenting work was meaningful and successful. Even amid grief and uncertainty about their future, parents can cling to this achievement as proof of their lasting impact. Successful parenting is not your child's ongoing dependence, but your own temporary obsolescence. A sense of successful parenting builds emotional space for other relationships that may have been overshadowed during the intensive care-giving years. But looking back is only half the story. To move forward, parents need tools to navigate emotions in real time.

Emotional Intelligence

Emotional intelligence is one of the most valuable skills at this stage.[5] The ability to recognise, understand, and manage your emotions while also responding thoughtfully to others' feelings is essential.

In the early days, self-awareness helps you notice subtle triggers: an untouched room, the absence of a daily text, or how certain seasons bring a sharper longing. It involves recognising that your emotions are valid responses to significant life changes, not signs of weakness or failure to adapt. It means understanding that grief and joy can exist together, and that missing your children doesn't lessen your pride in their independence.

Self-regulation relies on awareness, helping you respond to emotions without being overwhelmed, creating space for healthier coping strategies instead of sinking into sorrow and rumination. It's not about ignoring or suppressing how you feel; it's about pausing long enough to choose your response. When seeing your child's first diary brings tears, self-regulation might mean allowing the emotion to pass through you, observing the wave without being pulled under, then grounding yourself with a walk outside, a call to a friend, or a few deep breaths.

It might involve setting boundaries around spiralling thoughts, such as limiting late-night scrolling through old photos or gently redirecting conversations when they become repetitive loops of loss. For others, it consists of creating small practices like journaling, meditating, exercising, or simply pausing to name the feeling out loud, actions that transform emotion into manageable energy. Over time, these choices build resilience, showing that while you cannot control the feelings that arrive, you can influence how long they stay and how deeply they cut.

Where emotions shift rapidly between pride, grief, relief, and longing, self-regulation allows you to hold all these without judgment, giving you the steadiness to move forward rather than feeling paralysed by the past.

Empathy also plays a vital role. While your emotions might feel overwhelming, understanding your children's experiences, such as excitement, fear, or occasional homesickness, can strengthen your connection without overstepping boundaries. Recognising that they're navigating their own complex feelings about independence and separation helps maintain healthy relationships.

Perhaps most importantly, emotional intelligence fosters the strength to manage ambiguity. It allows you to hold pride and sadness simultaneously without feeling you must erase one to have the other, recognising that this challenging transition is also an opportunity for growth and rediscovery.

An Empty Nest Survival Kit

The following strategies can provide a roadmap for surviving the emotional landscape of the empty nest, which is covered in greater depth throughout the book.

Acknowledge the Reality of Your Feelings - The first and most important step is to validate your experience. Whether you feel devastated, relieved, confused, or a mix of all, these feelings are genuine responses to a significant life change. Avoid the temptation to judge yourself for how you "should" be feeling. Instead, practise self-compassion and recognise that adjustment takes time.

Create New Practices and Routines - The absence of child-centred routines can leave a void that feels over-whelming. Instead of trying to fill every moment, intentionally establish new habits that respect this phase of life. This might be a morning exercise routine, watching a movie, undertaking short courses after dinner, or a weekly activity solely for your enjoyment.

Gradually Reclaim Your Physical Space - Resist the urge to immediately convert your child's room or remove all traces of their presence. Allow yourself time to adjust to the visual reminders while slowly reclaiming space for your needs. This process should happen at your own pace, whether over weeks or months.

Build Relationships Beyond Parenting - Focus on strengthening bonds that aren't centred on your role as a parent. Reach out to old friends, join new groups, or deepen connections with partners, siblings, or extended family. These relationships offer emotional support and help define your identity outside motherhood.

Explore Postponed Dreams and Interests - This stage provides a valuable chance to revisit dreams or interests put aside during busy parenting years. Whether going back to education, taking up a creative hobby, or facing new challenges at work, this process can help reignite a sense of purpose and excitement about what's ahead.

Practice Staying Connected Without Overstepping - Learning to keep a bond with your adult children while respecting their independence is a continual skill. This might involve setting communication routines that suit both of you, showing genuine interest in their lives without being overbearing, and offering support without trying to fix their problems.

Seek Professional Support - Don't hesitate to seek expert help if the emotional toll becomes overwhelming or persistent. Counsellors, therapists, or support groups can offer valuable tools for processing grief, developing coping strategies, and managing this major life transition.

Be Patient with the Process - Remember that this adjustment is a journey, not a single event. Expect setbacks, celebrate small wins, and be patient with yourself as you move through this new chapter. Most people find that the intensity of tough emotions lessens over time, replaced by a renewed sense of purpose and potential.

The Dance of Return

Just as you've learned to cook for yourself or for two, the door opens again. Adult children return. Whether temporary or long-term, this return brings its own emotional challenges.[6] They come home with suitcases that smell of different laundry detergents, degrees that crinkle when unfolded, new passports, body art that you never liked or agreed to, and habits that

23

didn't develop under your watch. They return taller, older, changed, yet somehow still yours.

The house fills again with forgotten memories: shower doors sliding at midnight, keys dropping onto the counter, conversations that drift from room to room. But there's no emotional script for mothering an adult who shares your Wi-Fi password but not your daily life. The rules have changed, but nobody provided the new handbook. You must learn to mother without managing, love without leading, and care without controlling. It's the most complicated choreography you'll ever master.

The boomerang generation, prompted by economic pressures, career shifts, or life changes, has led to these returns becoming more common. For parents accustomed to the quiet of an empty nest, their return can feel both reassuring and awkward. Chapter 4 explores this theme in more detail.

A Journey in Different Languages

The emotional landscape of the empty nest is shaped by departures, changing identities, and sometimes unexpected returns. Whether your child has left, come back, or never quite gone, the roles are shifting, and so are you.

Recognising that your experience is very personal yet broadly shared means looking beyond individual stories to the wider patterns that influence us all. To achieve this, we need to challenge the powerful ideology underpinning many of our assumptions about the empty nest.

Hearing the stories of women around the world reminds us that this shift, though tough, is a new start. It is a gateway to discovering who we are when we're no longer needed in the same ways. The woman who waited beneath the sounds of school shoes, homework papers, and busy kitchens has always been there. But if we see the empty nest as a void, we risk missing the opportunities it offers. It's a chance to rediscover dreams, strengthen other connections, and become someone shaped by motherhood but not limited to it.

The next chapter revisits this cultural story in greater detail. Why is such a universal experience kept hidden within individual homes rather than recognised as a shared human experience? How might we develop frameworks to support significant life changes with potential mental health implications, workplace policies, and community programs tailored specifically for this stage? And what could shift if we brought the empty nest experience out of the shadows and into public awareness?

Reflections and Practices

Individual Reflection Prompts
Identity and Self-Discovery

- Write a letter to the woman you were before you became a mother. What would you tell her about the journey ahead?
- Describe a moment from your pre-children life when you felt most genuinely yourself. What elements of that person are you curious to rediscover?
-

Creative Journalling Exercises
Future Visioning

- Write a postcard to yourself from five years in the future. What are you doing?

- List 10 things you've always wanted to try but never had time for. Circle the three that spark the most curiosity.

Guided Writing Exercises
The Room Exercise

- Sit in your child's former room (or imagine it). Write for 10 minutes about what you notice: the light, objects, silence, and memories. Don't try to make meaning—just record.

Letters You'll Never Send

- Write a letter to the mother you were during the busiest years, acknowledging everything she carried.

Key Takeaway
Mapping this emotional landscape isn't just about surviving the change. It's about seeing it as an opportunity to step out, find new possibilities, and learn from the inherent challenges they bring.

Chapter 2

Why the Empty Nest Matters

Actually, Mum, the book says you should let us fail sometimes. She looked up from the dishes to see her middle daughter holding one of the parenting guides she'd borrowed from the local library, the ones she'd been meaning to read for weeks. The books were stacked on a table beside the couch. She'd hoped their wisdom might offer some good tips. But her daughters always got to them first, flipping through pages, learning parenting tips and hacks, sometimes correcting her with quotes from books she hadn't yet read. They were growing up, learning about the world beyond the farm and probably never really thinking they wouldn't be with her forever.

The books were intended to guide her, yet the children always seemed a step ahead. One daughter, an avid reader, once teased that she was "in denial" long before the phrase became popular. And she was right. She never planned to become an empty nester; how could she understand a stage of life she hadn't yet experienced? Only later did she realise how deep this transition could be. She didn't have all the answers, as few parents do, but she sensed that many were asking the same questions in silence.

According to the Australian Bureau of Statistics, children leaving home is a common, normal, and significant part of life.[1] It is common because most children grow up and leave; normal because it happens in nearly every family; significant because it changes identity, relationships, and community in ways few other life stages do. Personal and social conversations about the empty nest remain unspoken despite its widespread occurrence.

The empty nest crosses every demographic boundary. It does not discriminate based on social class, education, cultural background, or location. It impacts most families worldwide, yet each family experiences it as a unique private event. Such universal experiences should not be faced alone. It deserves recognition as a significant transition from being a daily caregiver to entering a new and unfamiliar phase.

While we celebrate children's achievements and independence, we rarely acknowledge the cost to parents or provide support for this major life upheaval. The silence around the empty nest experience extends beyond individual families to broader societal conversations. This cultural blind spot leaves many feeling isolated in their struggle, unsure whether their feelings are normal or excessive.

To continue treating it as a private struggle rather than a shared milestone is to overlook one of the most significant yet least named transitions of modern family life. Although the term "empty nest" exists, the experience it represents has never been fully named, authorised, or honoured in our cultural language. Recognising it as a public health and wellbeing issue would not only validate the emotional realities parents face but also open pathways for preventative support, reducing the hidden costs of loneliness, depression, and social disconnection.

Part of the challenge is that while we have begun to recognise the empty nest as a social and health concern, we still lack the collective rituals and cultural scripts that would help parents acknowledge and navigate it together. There are no rituals to mark its arrival, no ceremonies to validate the transition, and no social scripts to guide parents through it. This silence isn't accidental. It reflects outdated expectations, and institutional oversights. The cost of ignoring this stage is high, especially for women, but so is the potential when it is recognised. When society names and normalises this transition, it unlocks the potential for growth, connection, and renewed purpose in midlife. This chapter explores why the empty nest remains unspoken, why naming it matters, and how silence carries risks and opportunities.

The Historical Making of Empty Houses

The idea of the empty nest is relatively recent. Throughout history, it seemed impractical and unnatural for children to leave home permanently around age 18. Families typically lived and worked together across generations, with the home as the centre of economic activity, social connection, and mutual care.

The empty nest syndrome was first recognised clinically in the 1970s, arising from research by psychologists examining midlife changes in women. Researchers noted a pattern of depressive symptoms, loss of purpose, and identity crises occurring when children left home. These symptoms were severe enough to require clinical attention. The term "syndrome" itself implied a medical condition needing diagnosis and treatment, framing what was a natural life change as a possible pathological state.

The timing of this clinical identification is significant. These were the same decades that saw the rise of suburban nuclear families, increased mobility for work and education, and the cultural elevation of individual achievement over collective belonging.

The syndrome emerged not because parents suddenly began feeling sadness when children left, but because the entire structure of family life had shifted. For the first time in history, large numbers of mothers, particularly middle-class women who had dedicated decades primarily to child-rearing, faced an abrupt end to their primary role without the multigenerational support systems or ongoing family collaboration that had previously cushioned such transitions.

Early clinical literature often pathologised mothers specifically, sometimes describing empty nest syndrome as a failure to adapt or a sign of unhealthy attachment. This gendered framing ignored broader social factors: the isolation of nuclear families, limited career options for women who had taken time out of the workforce, and cultural messages that equated good mothering with self-sacrifice. The "syndrome", therefore, was as much a product of social structure as individual psychology.

In pre-industrial Australia, adult children often stayed in or near the family home, helping with household income and caring for ageing parents. The Indigenous Australian concept of Country, where connection to place spans generations, sharply contrasts the Western ideal of individual mobility and independence. First Nations cultures regard belonging as collective and ongoing, with responsibility flowing both ways.

The shift toward nuclear family isolation accelerated after World War II. Government policies encouraged suburban homeownership, new appliances promised to make housework more efficient, and the post-war economic boom enabled families to survive on a single income. By the 1960s and 70s, women's magazines began featuring articles about "empty nest syndrome," often describing it in medical terms as a form of depression that needed treatment.

A peculiar paradox emerged: Parents were expected to raise children to be independent enough to leave, prosperous enough to thrive independently, and emotionally resilient enough not to need ongoing family support. Yet this assumed stable employment, affordable housing, and clear career paths, conditions already eroding as the empty nest became embedded in culture.

Why We Don't Talk About It
The Good Parent Trap
Modern society has constructed a complex framework around parenting that makes it nearly impossible to discuss the transition to an empty nest openly. At its core is an idealised view of parenthood as inherently selfless, where good parents prioritise their children's needs above their own without question or complaint. In this framework, expressing sadness when your children leave can feel like admitting failure rather than a natural response. Admitting grief over a child's departure seems to conflict with the very essence of good parenting,

forming a cultural double bind where parents must choose between being honest about their feelings and seeking social approval for their parenting achievements.

This stigma is particularly powerful because it attacks parents' core identities and sense of competence, making them less likely to seek support or admit their difficulties even to themselves. Parents internalise the message that struggling with this transition shows either a failure to prepare their children for independence or selfish attachment to children who should be free to live their own lives. The taboo surrounding parental vulnerability is particularly intense for mothers, who face social pressure to be endlessly nurturing and supportive while rarely revealing their own needs for help or understanding.

The pressure affects both mothers and fathers, though differently. Men encounter masculine norms that entirely discourage emotional expression. David, whose daughter moved across the country for work, found himself struggling with unexpected grief: *I couldn't even tell my wife how much I missed her. What kind of father misses his kid when she's succeeding?* Another father told me, *I'm proud she flew, but I didn't realise the house would echo like this.*

The Inheritance

Such modern silence is rooted in generational patterns influencing how families manage emotional transitions. Many current empty nesters were brought up by parents who viewed emotional vulnerability as a weakness and private struggles as personal failures to be endured quietly. This inheritance constructs a culture where parents lack models for healthy emotional processing during significant life changes. Parents may instinctively retreat into privacy, convinced that speaking about emptiness or loneliness only exposes fragility rather than strength. The outcome is a lack of conversation; parents feel something deeply human but rarely voice it. Unlike major life events like divorce or job loss that cause sudden ruptures, the empty nest gradually and invisibly unfolds.

A slow unravelling makes the shift easy to minimise for those living through it and for outsiders who may not notice its weight. Because the transition is so incremental, it is often dismissed as a natural evolution rather than recognised as a profound life stage. The silence grows not because the experience is small, but because it hides in plain sight.

The Social Media Mirage

Social media often presents a cheerful side. Parents upload graduation photos, move-in shots, and celebrations of their newfound freedom while deliberately hiding feelings of grief, loneliness, or identity confusion. Such selective sharing gives an erroneous impression that most parents transition smoothly, which can heighten shame and loneliness for those privately struggling with their own experiences.

Erin scrolled through Facebook after dropping her daughter at university, seeing post after post of beaming parents celebrating their empty nest adventures. She closed the app, feeling broken and alone, wondering why she couldn't muster the same enthusiasm for her suddenly calm house.

Without social recognition or support, parents often

experience prolonged adjustment periods and unnecessary psychological distress, missing opportunities for growth that community backing could provide.

Naming Matters

When something has no name, it has no shape. It cannot be measured, studied, or supported. It simply dissolves into the background noise of life. As Brené Brown reminds us, shame derives its power from being unspeakable. The same is true for life transitions: What we fail to name, we fail to honour. What we fail to honour, we fail to heal.

Millions of women enter the empty nest every year, and society looks the other way, not because this experience doesn't matter, but because we've never been taught to see it. When the daily demands of motherhood fade, so does the cultural value we place on those who perform them. This silence isn't just emotional; it has real consequences.

Naming the empty nest as a legitimate life transition is an act of advocacy. When we say it out loud, we make space for compassion. We create room for conversations in families, friendships, workplaces, and communities. We need more representations of this life stage in the media, not just the stereotypical "weepy mother" or the carefree woman dancing alone in her empty kitchen, but nuanced, honest, varied depictions of what it feels like. We need stories that show the contradiction: the pride and the grief sitting side by side, the freedom and the disorientation coexisting in the same afternoon.

When Systems Fail to See

This silence becomes costly when institutions designed to support families, such as healthcare, workplaces, community, and social services, fail to recognise this transition adequately. This oversight deepens the cultural silence, creating multiple layers of dismissal that leave parents without adequate resources or recognition.

Healthcare providers rarely ask about the emotional impact of children leaving home during routine visits. A GP's simple question, such as 'Any big family changes lately?', can open the right doorway. This means depression, anxiety, or identity confusion related to the empty nest may be attributed to other causes or dismissed as normal ageing. Mood changes during this period are frequently misdiagnosed, leading to inappropriate treatment approaches and prolonged adjustment difficulties.[2]

Because the empty nest often coincides with menopause, career transitions, or eldercare responsibilities, researchers call it a "pile-up effect"[3] where several stressors hit simultaneously. Healthcare providers may focus on hormonal changes while missing the grief of role transition or address work stress while overlooking family adjustment challenges.

Employment settings often assume that empty nesters automatically gain more freedom and availability. Managers might expect longer work hours or more flexibility from employees whose children have left home without recognising that this transition can temporarily affect focus, motivation, or emotional stability. Maya recalled her boss assuming she'd pick up late meetings now. But she barely slept and needed time to find her feet after her child left.

Professional environments that fail to acknowledge this adjustment period may lose valuable employees who withdraw from career engagement while struggling with unrecognised challenges. Women in their prime earning years may reduce professional involvement or decline advancement opportunities during this vulnerable time, representing a significant loss of talent and experience.

These overlapping silences carry serious consequences that flow far beyond individual families, creating ripple effects that impact economic productivity, mental health systems, and even the next generation. Unaddressed emotional distress can trigger a cascade of mental health challenges that extend well beyond the initial empty nest adjustment period. What begins as natural grief about role change can develop into chronic stress, depression, and anxiety when parents lack recognition and support for their experience. These psychological impacts often manifest in physical health problems such as cardiovascular issues, immune system suppression, and sleep disorders,[4] which represent both individual suffering and substantial public healthcare costs.

The ripple effect doesn't end with parents. When parents grapple with unacknowledged identity shifts, it influences their relationships with their adult children, who may feel guilty about their parents' unhappiness or unsure about how to set healthy boundaries. Adult children often say they feel responsible for their parents' emotional state during this time, leading to anxiety and relationship tension that can last for years. Our children cannot be held accountable for their parents' unrest, nor should they carry the burden of our unresolved change. The work of healing and redefining ourselves is ours alone. Doing so gives them the freedom to live their lives more fully.

The Economic Toll of Oversight

The failure to recognise the empty nest transition carries significant economic consequences that remain largely hidden from public view.

This represents a profound loss of human capital precisely when societies need experienced leadership most. Empty nesters possess decades of crisis management, organisational skills, and institutional knowledge. When they withdraw from professional engagement due to unsupported personal transitions, the economic impact ripples through industries and communities that lose their expertise and mentorship.

The healthcare costs associated with untreated mental health impacts during this transition add another layer of economic burden. Preventive support during the adjustment period could significantly reduce long-term treatment costs while improving quality of life and productivity. Beyond these institutional and financial consequences, how parents navigate this transition creates ripples that extend into the next generation's understanding of resilience, vulnerability, and change.

Intergenerational Modelling

How parents handle this transition teaches adult children crucial lessons about resilience, ageing gracefully, and sustaining relationships through change. When parents struggle in silence, they inadvertently teach their children that major life transitions should be endured alone and that asking for help signals weakness.

Josie watched her mother withdraw into herself when Josie left for university. She never talked about her feelings, insisting everything was "fine" despite her apparent sadness. Twenty years later, Josie repeated those same patterns when her daughter moved out, only to realise she was following a learned script. She understood that she was teaching her daughter the same lesson her mother taught her: that mothers aren't allowed to need anything.

Conversely, modelling healthy adjustment (seeking support, expressing emotions, embracing new opportunities) demonstrates that change can be met with authenticity and strength. Zac told his son directly, *I'm really proud of you, and I'm also finding the house too quiet right now. I'm figuring out what comes next for me.* His son later said that the conversation shaped how he approached his own career transition: *You showed me it's okay to acknowledge when something is hard, even when it's good.*

Parents who actively rebuild their identities demonstrate that life transitions can be catalysts for growth rather than merely losses to be endured. Breaking the cultural silence becomes an act of intergenerational teaching, signalling that this transition matters enough to warrant attention and support.

When parents show their children how to maintain connection through shifting roles, whether in marriage, friendship, or community, they model the importance of tending relationships across every stage of life. These intergenerational patterns emerge partly because the empty nest contains a fundamental contradiction that makes it challenging to navigate openly.

The Paradox of Successful Parenting

The empty nest's most psychologically complex aspect is that it simultaneously signifies both triumph and loss;[5] the achievement of parenting's primary goal of raising independent, capable adults, while also bringing grief and emptiness to parents. This paradox means that the most successful parents often experience the sharpest sense of absence when children leave. The better the job parents have done in creating secure, confident young adults, the more fully those children will thrive, leaving parents grappling with the bittersweet nature of their success.

For women whose identities have been mainly built around caregiving and maternal roles, the empty nest presents a fundamental challenge to their sense of self and purpose.[6] Decades of decision-making based on children's needs, schedules organised around family requirements, and social connections formed through parenting activities suddenly become irrelevant. Rather than viewing this shift in identity as simply adapting to change, it is more effective to see it as reconstructing a sense of self that may have been dormant for twenty or more years. It therefore needs the same support and recognition given to other major identity transitions. While this paradox is psychologically complex, it also has potential for transformation. The loss, which feels destabilising, can lay the groundwork for profound renewal.

Hidden Opportunities for Renaissance

Parents often describe "meeting themselves again" after decades of being primarily defined by their relationships to others. This rediscovery process can reveal interests, talents, and aspects of personality that were suppressed or unexplored during intensive parenting years, leading to greater authenticity, self-awareness, and personal fulfilment.

Empty nesters are uniquely positioned for career reinvention and professional growth. They possess experience, wisdom, and newfound time flexibility to drive remarkable professional achievements. Many discover that skills developed through parenting (crisis management, multitasking, negotiation, and leadership) translate directly to professional success. Without the constraints of children's schedules, empty nesters can pursue education, accept challenging assignments, travel for work, or launch entrepreneurial ventures that were previously impossible. These themes will be explored further in other chapters.

Couples who successfully navigate the empty nest phase often report experiencing deeper intimacy and a stronger partnership than during their active parenting years. Without the constant interruptions and competing priorities of children's needs, couples can reconnect as individuals, rebuild romantic bonds, and pursue shared interests that may have been difficult to undertake while managing family responsibilities. This renaissance in marriage strengthens relationships to a level that can be even more fulfilling than in their early years together. Relationships will be examined in later chapters.

The empty nest transition also allows parent-child relationships to evolve into adult friendships characterised by mutual respect, shared interests, and voluntary rather than obligatory connection. Parents who successfully navigate this transition often discover that their relationships with adult children become deeper and more satisfying than the hierarchical relationships of active parenting.

How Society Overlooks Parent Transitions

Society's emphasis on children's achievements often misses the parallel changes parents experience during these milestones.[7] When a child graduates from university, much attention is given to the student's successes and prospects. Meanwhile, little consideration is paid to parents going through the end of their daily parenting roles.

Take a minute to reflect on graduation ceremonies: Cameras focus on the graduate walking across the stage while parents sit in the audience, their profound transition invisible to everyone, including themselves. The graduate receives congratulations, advice for their next chapter, and social recognition of their achievement. The parents get a brief "You must be so proud" before attention shifts to the young person's future. One mother recalled everyone asking about her daughter's next step after the graduation ceremony, but no one asked about hers.

This oversight exposes deeper cultural values that prioritise youth and achievement while undervaluing the experiences of those who helped shape these successes. Parents become background figures in the very stories they've spent decades shaping. Such invisibility runs through nearly every milestone. Wedding planning centres on the couple, while parents quietly process their shift from central to extended family members. Career celebrations focus on young professionals, while parents who supported them through years of study receive perfunctory acknowledgment at best.

The language itself reveals the bias. We have countless terms for young people in transition: graduates, newlyweds, emerging adults, young professionals. For parents at the same juncture, we have only "empty nester," a term that defines them by absence rather than what they are moving toward. Imagine calling university graduates "newly unemployed students" or newlyweds "former singles." Yet we accept this deficit language for parents without question.

Compare this deficit model to other major life transitions. Retirement comes with parties and speeches that honour decades of contribution. Marriages begin with ceremonies that publicly mark commitment. Even adolescence receives acknowledgment through graduations and coming-of-age traditions. Despite affecting nearly every parent and lasting potentially decades, the empty nest receives none of this recognition.

Until we develop a cultural space for parents' transitions to be seen and named, we continue to treat parenthood as purely instrumental rather than a profound human experience worthy of honour. The empty nest matters because parents matter, not just as facilitators of the next generation, but as people whose experiences deserve to be witnessed and supported. This cultural oversight isn't merely insensitive; it carries tangible consequences that affect individuals, families, and entire communities. Yet the solution doesn't require a massive systemic overhaul. Recognition can begin with surprisingly simple shifts.

Placing it firmly on the social and political agenda involves integrating empty nest awareness into healthcare frameworks as a significant life change with potential mental health effects, developing workplace policies that support employees during this transition rather than exploiting their perceived availability, and creating targeted community programs specifically designed for this stage. Progressive employers are starting to recognise that supporting employees through significant life changes enhances retention and productivity much more than expecting immediate increased availability.

The silence around the empty nest benefits no one. If you are a parent approaching this transition, acknowledge your feelings without shame. If you know someone in this stage, ask how they're doing and genuinely mean it. Make room for this conversation, particularly if you work in healthcare, education, or community services. And if you've already gone through the empty nest phase, share your story. Your honesty can be a lifeline for those still navigating it. Silence isolates parents during a vulnerable time, wastes human potential, and extends unnecessary suffering while showing poor adjustment strategies to the next generation. By giving this experience language, we validate it. Recognising its costs prevents needless isolation. And by viewing it as an opportunity, we unlock energy, wisdom, and love that benefit parents and entire communities.

The next chapter turns from silence to stories, showing how culture shapes what families do when children leave and what those moments mean. From Western ideals of independence to traditions of interdependence and continuity, we will explore how different love, loyalty, and family scripts reshape the experience of our children's departure. These stories remind us that the empty nest experience is carried in our world's language, rituals, and expectations.

Reflections and Practices

Individual Reflection Prompt

- What assumptions did you hold about the "empty nest" before it happened (or before reading this chapter)? Which of those assumptions have proven true, and which have surprised you?

Awareness Activity

- Notice the cultural messages you've absorbed about parenting and independence. Jot down one or two phrases you've heard (*Good parents let go easily, Mothers should be selfless*). How have these shaped the way you see yourself in this transition?

Guided Writing Exercise

- Write a short reflection: "The silence around the empty nest has meant that I..." Allow yourself to finish the sentence in many ways without editing.

Key Takeaway

The empty nest matters because it is both universal and unspoken. Recognising it, acknowledging cultural silences, and starting to share your own experience are the first steps to turning this transition from a private challenge into a shared human story.

Chapter 3

Culture and Letting Go

*S*he stood in the driveway, keys still in hand, staring at the bright starlit night sky. Nothing marked the moment, just an empty house behind her and stars that had witnessed this same scene play out across countless driveways. She wondered how many other mothers were navigating this threshold under this same constellation, each carrying different stories about what it meant when children left home. Culture, she realises, doesn't just influence how we feel about this transition. It determines whether we even recognise it as a transition at all.

Under these same stars, a thousand goodbyes unfold, and none are wrong. If you're reading this, you might find that your experience of children leaving home doesn't match what you expected, or what others told you to expect. This chapter explores how culture shapes your expectations and emotional experience when children leave home. Through stories from different families, you'll see how values of independence, interdependence, and adaptation influence the meaning you give to this transition and how you physically experience it. Instead of accepting the idea of a single empty nest experience, you'll discover various cultural ways of loving and staying connected, approaches that modern economic realities and multicultural Australian life are continually transforming.

The Scripts We Inherit

What you think of as natural is deeply cultural.[1] Cultural norms and values shape parenting practices, creating inherited scripts about family, independence, and love that influence what you expect and how you feel when the moment arrives.

The language you inherit shapes what you believe is possible. English-speaking cultures have developed extensive vocabulary around independence: "launching," "letting go," "empty nest," and "failure to launch," all suggest movement away from family connection as the primary goal of development.[2] Other languages offer different frameworks. Mandarin concepts of filial piety encompass ongoing responsibility and connection across generations.[3] Arabic cultures speak of family honour, where individual achievements reflect collective family identity rather than representing separation.[4]

These aren't just words; they're maps of how love manifests. In multicultural Australia, many carry more than one map. Families must navigate between different frameworks, creating hybrid approaches that honour heritage while adapting to contemporary realities. Still, inherited scripts become most obvious when they clash. When one cultural map says stay and another says go, parents face confusion as well as contradiction.

The reality of those maps becomes clear in everyday life. When Fatima's son Ahmed moved out at twenty-two to share a flat near his engineering job, reactions from her

Iraqi community were quick and pointed. A neighbour asked directly why he wasn't staying until marriage and what had gone wrong. Fatima felt like she'd failed him somehow, even though his Australian friends saw him as independent and successful.

Ahmed's departure symbolised family breakdown or Western influence in Fatima's Iraqi community. Among her Australian colleagues, it represented healthy growth and good parenting. She found herself caught between two stories, neither of which felt complete.

Fatima noticed hot flushes around the same time. Her doctor said they were due to menopause, but she wondered if her body was reacting to the stress of feeling torn between two sets of expectations. In Iraq, her mother had lived with the family until she passed away. Here, she was meant to embrace independence. Her body carried the tension between worlds, showing how cultural conflict can influence physical symptoms alongside physiological changes. Her body kept score of conflicting expectations, reminding us that culture is felt as much as it is believed. Cultural dissonance looks like this: not just an intellectual debate, but a physical burden expressed through heat, tension, and sleepless nights.

This crossroad of culture and biology unveils something vital: the empty nest isn't just an emotional experience but a physical one, moulded by the stories societies tell about what good mothers do and what healthy families look like. When those stories clash, bodies bear the contradiction.

Living Together: The Persistence of Connection

Linda's experience tells a different story altogether. A second-generation Chinese Australian mother from Melbourne, she never felt the loneliness her Western friends described. Her daughter Jenny didn't leave home before marriage, and even after her wedding, the young couple moved into the extended family's house. Linda's Australian friends kept asking when Jenny would fly the nest, seeming to think she was fostering dependency. But in her family, this arrangement showed love and practical wisdom. The question for Linda was simple: why would they want Jenny to struggle alone with rent and childcare when the family could support each other?

When Jenny's first baby arrived, three generations shared in the caregiving. Linda's mother helped with night feeds while Linda managed daycare, and Jenny went back to work. The idea of an empty nest didn't suit their reality. Linda never felt that loneliness, but she also never had the chance to rediscover herself as her friends described.

Linda's journey through menopause took place within a continued sense of purpose and family ties. Instead of losing her identity, she saw her role gradually evolve within an established framework. The same biological processes, when viewed through different cultural perspectives, resulted in very different lived experiences.

People from cultures that value interdependence might be confused by friends who talk about getting their life back or rediscovering themselves. The experience might be more about changing roles within ongoing relationships rather than starting anew. Even families that successfully keep their cultural traditions face forces beyond their control. Geography and economics don't care about tradition. They rewrite scripts whether families agree or not.

Distance and Economic Reality

While some families follow cultural scripts about staying close, others are shaped more by geographic and economic forces that can completely override cultural preferences. Leah from Tasmania learned to maintain connections differently when geography and economics made traditional closeness impossible. Her daughter moved to Melbourne for university and stayed for work, visiting twice a year when flights were affordable. Her son moved to Perth to work in mining, creating distances that required reimagining what family connection could look like.

People assumed Leah must be lonely, but she learned to connect differently. Her children took family values with them when they left. Jess runs a community garden in her Melbourne neighbourhood. Tom organises safety training for new workers. They're still nurturing people, just in different places.

Leah's story reflects a growing trend in contemporary Australia: living miles apart but staying close through shared values instead of shared space. The children might have taken themselves elsewhere physically, but they carry their upbringing with them wherever they go. Sometimes, the nest isn't empty; it's expanded beyond the walls of just one house.

Megan, a childcare educator from suburban Brisbane, didn't face cultural push and pull. Hers was simply an empty house. She described her family as ordinary, without big traditions to rely on. She walked the dog longer, cooked less, and found that Saturday mornings could be hers. Ordinariness is a culture too, and that reality is just as valid as any other approach.

Those facing geographic separation from their children are not alone in needing to rethink what connection means. Economic pressures shaping family transitions cannot be overlooked. More than ever, family support or its absence has become a key factor in housing outcomes for young people. This reality creates new stories where adult children stay at home not by choice or cultural tradition, but out of necessity.

When Children Return

Adapting cultural expectations becomes even more complicated when circumstances completely override personal preferences. Serena, from regional Queensland, thought she understood the timeline only to have life rewrite the script. Her son left for university at eighteen, then spent two years travelling overseas. She had adjusted to the empty house and started enjoying her own company, turning his gym into an art studio. Then the 2020 pandemic hit, and he returned home at twenty-four. Researchers call these accordion families, which expand and contract as life changes.[5]

Suddenly, Serena had to redo everything. The gym she had turned into an art studio became his bedroom again. She felt guilty for resenting the change and adjusting so quickly to his absence. Serena's experience illustrates how the empty nest is often fleeting, requiring ongoing adaptation rather than a single switch.

The physical impact was immediate. Her sleep patterns

fell out of sync again just as she had grown used to having her own space and rhythm. Her body had to readjust to sharing space and schedules. Even her digestion changed with the shift back to cooking for two. The accordion didn't just expand and contract; it played an entirely different tune each time, and her body had to relearn the melody. Her experience demonstrates how family transitions affect us physically and emotionally.

Serena's story highlights a rising Australian trend. Challenges in finding affordable housing can delay a young person's decision to leave the parental home. More adaptable arrangements are replacing the traditional linear story of leaving home once and for all.

Making Your Own Ceremonies

Reading other women's stories, you see how each one manages her emotions and the cultural expectations around them. Each was expected to perform a version of motherhood that didn't match her real life. Most had to find meaning because the usual guides were missing.

Western cultures have largely abandoned meaningful rituals around children leaving home, which contributes to the disorientation many parents feel.[6] While milestones like graduation or moving day are celebrated, the wider emotional shift within families often goes unrecognised. Unlike births, weddings, or funerals, this passage occurs without ceremony, leaving parents to navigate it privately. It might often mean you end up planning your own ceremonies in isolation.

Maria, from Perth, created her own tradition. She made a photo book for each child's childhood and gave it to them when they moved out. Then she planted a tree in the backyard. It felt like she was honouring their growth and marking a new chapter. Another Greek Australian mother started preparing her son's favourite foods and delivering them to his new apartment each week, turning traditional hospitality into a way to stay connected despite the distance.

In contrast, Indigenous Australian cultures have long held meaningful initiation ceremonies to mark the shift from childhood to adulthood within their communities. These traditions recognise that such milestones require witness, support, and collective acknowledgment.[7] They reveal a deep human desire for recognition that change is important.

Whether you see your children leaving as a loss or a transformation, whether temporary or permanent, these moments deserve acknowledgment and support. Most families don't follow a single clear pattern. They're more than likely blending different approaches as they go.

The Australian Context

In multicultural Australia, most of us are bilingual in a sense of belonging. Our multicultural reality makes hybrid approaches the norm rather than the exception.[8] We don't just tolerate cultural differences; instead, we embody them in our homes, bodies, and the space between what our parents expect and what our children need. Cross-cultural understanding and respect, along with fostering inclusive practices that recognise and value the richness of cultural diversity, become vital as families navigate multiple cultural frameworks simultaneously.

If you're navigating between different cultural expectations, you're doing important work. Fatima eventually learned to balance her Iraqi values of family closeness with Australian values of individual development, fostering conversations with Ahmed that honoured his independence and their ongoing connection. Linda found ways to celebrate Jenny's growing autonomy within their interdependent family structure. Leah developed new methods to maintain connections across distances. Serena set flexible boundaries that could adapt to changing circumstances.

Each woman's journey reveals the ongoing process of cultural translation, as she adapts inherited stories about family, love, and responsibility to fit contemporary Australian life. This process is neither simple nor finished but shows families' creative ability to honour their past while responding to current circumstances.

Honouring Your Path

The meaning of an empty home varies widely. It can represent freedom, bring sorrow, signal new opportunities, or cause deep cultural tensions. You might experience these feelings at different times, even within the same day. What remains consistent across cultures is that change is important. Adjusting your inherited stories to match your experiences requires personal bravery and cultural support. In Australia's diverse society, recognising different ways of managing family changes reminds us that while emotions may seem universal, our interpretation of them is shaped by our cultural stories.

The empty nest symbolises a range of experiences all sharing the same name. And that's exactly how it should be. There's no single way to handle love, loss, and family changes.

It's a continuous process of adapting, honouring, and passing your stories forward. Recognising your inherited cultural narrative is the first step in rewriting it to suit the life you want now. Whether you're celebrating newfound freedom, mourning the end of daily mothering, adjusting to economic realities, or forging new connections across distances, you're part of a larger story of families adapting and thriving in modern Australia.

Whether your cultural script told you to hold on, let go, celebrate, or grieve, the moment eventually arrives. When it does, practical preparation becomes an act of self-kindness. In the next chapter, we turn inward to the deeply personal work of preparing both home and heart, because knowing your cultural story is one thing; being ready to live it is another.

Reflections and Practices

Individual Reflection Prompts

- What stories did you inherit about good parenting when children leave home? Independence? Loyalty? Something else?
- Think about your parents or grandparents. How did their generation handle children leaving home? How does your experience compare?

Cultural Awareness Activity

- List two cultural messages you've absorbed about what it means when children leave (e.g., *They should move out young to be independent. Children should stay close until marriage*). Do these messages help or hinder your own experience?

Try rewriting one of those cultural scripts in your own words to fit your reality better.

Creative Journaling Exercise – Inventing Ritual
- What might it have looked like if there had been a ceremony when your child left home? Who would have been there? What words, symbols, or actions would have helped mark the moment?
- If your child returned home, what ritual might acknowledge that transition, too?

Key Takeaway

There is no single script. Every family carries cultural stories about independence, loyalty, and love. Part of the empty nest journey is learning which stories still serve you, and which you might need to adapt or rewrite to match your contemporary reality.

PART II:

LIVING THE TRANSITION

Chapter 4

Preparing the Home,
Preparing the Heart

*S*he was physically prepared. *Her daughters had been away at boarding school for years, mastering routines and managing decisions without her nearby. By the time they left home for good, they were capable and ready. But something shifted when she understood they would not return permanently. The moment marked the beginning of a new reality, a journey to explore her purpose beyond motherhood.*

Although she maintained strong bonds with her daughters, the distance felt heavier than anticipated. Phone calls and occasional visits provided comfort, but the separation lingered. In that space, she noted how deeply motherhood had shaped her, perhaps more than any academic or professional accomplishment ever did.

She wished she had prepared more thoughtfully, both practically and emotionally. Conversations before they left about how their relationships might change, or visualisations of life beyond active motherhood, could have eased the transition.

She wandered through the house. Outdated clothes, half-folded bed linen, and sports trophies lined the shelves just as they'd left them. It wasn't time to pack anything away, not emo-

tionally, not physically. Not ever. She hoped they were coming back to her.

The truth is that you probably won't see it coming. We're still caught up in the daily rhythm of active parenting when the first signs appear: a meal they cook without help, a solo drive to training, or a big decision made without asking for your opinion. These moments of independence are both victories and reminders, a powerful contradiction at the core of parenting. Our children's departure often feels like something that happens *to* us rather than something we can prepare *for*. But the transition doesn't have to catch us completely off guard.

With careful planning on two levels, we can change how we approach this shift: preparing ourselves emotionally for what lies ahead and organising our homes by equipping our children with the practical skills they'll require. Practically, we might ask: Do they know how to do laundry? Can they manage money? Will they make good decisions? Can they make a nutritious meal? These essential questions represent only half of the preparation needed. The other half involves preparing ourselves and our hearts for the profound shift in our daily lives. Equipping our children for independence while strengthening our emotional foundation begins while our children are still at home.[1]

This chapter explores how to approach both sides of this preparation thoughtfully, so that when the departure moment arrives, you feel ready rather than blindsided. Here's the truth: teaching your child to do laundry is easier than training yourself to stop being needed. But both require the same deliberate practice, patience with imperfection, and trust in the process.

Preparing the Home

Across cultures and contexts, the emotional and logistical tasks of preparing children for independence are widely shared. While systems differ, the fundamentals remain consistent: documents, life skills, and confidence-building. While our children still live under our roof, we have countless opportunities to enhance their practical readiness for independent living. This benefits their success and our peace of mind. Knowing they can manage life's practicalities makes the emotional farewell much easier. As part of this preparation, it's important to recognise that independence today looks different from a generation ago. Practical readiness now includes confidently and securely managing life's essentials online.

Digital-First Administrative Foundations

Today's young adults navigate a primarily digital world. Start with the essentials they need to handle modern adult life: setting up government online accounts for Medicare and tax purposes, understanding digital banking and mobile payment apps, obtaining digital IDS where available, and creating secure password management systems. Help them learn about government apps for managing tax matters and accessing social services, state-specific apps for vehicle registration and licensing, and how to safely store and access digital copies of important documents. Encourage creating a shared digital folder with scanned copies of vital documents they can access from anywhere.

Many parents now find it useful to develop a collaborative adulting checklist using shared document platforms. This might include budgeting basics with expense-tracking apps, understanding rental applications via property websites, navigating public transport apps, and learning fundamental cooking skills with online tutorials or meal kit services for practice.

Modern Life Skills Development

The most effective way to prepare them is by gradually giving them responsibility for daily tasks, while you remain available to guide and troubleshoot. Let them handle their own laundry entirely, including the inevitable messes. Use grocery delivery occasionally to plan and shop for family meals. Have them manage their banking through mobile apps, book medical appointments online, and handle conflict resolution in digital spaces.

One mother recalled her daughter's first attempt at online grocery shopping: She described her daughter accidentally ordering 12 rolls of expensive hand towels instead of one. The daughter has since learned to double-check quantities and read product descriptions carefully. Her mother says she's now the most careful online shopper she knows. These learning experiences build genuine competence through manageable mistakes in a low-stakes environment.

Beyond these practical tasks, young adults need confidence in interpersonal situations that parents have previously managed. Practice having them make appointments by phone, handle complaints about faulty purchases, and navigate difficult conversations with service providers. These interactions build self-advocacy skills they'll need when dealing with landlords, employers, or healthcare providers independently. Encourage them to resolve conflicts with siblings or friends without parental mediation by learning to communicate their needs clearly and negotiate fair solutions. Most importantly, let them make mistakes.

Financial Literacy

Teaching practical money management now covers understanding digital currencies, recognising online scams, and managing digital subscriptions. Government financial education websites, personal finance podcasts, and budgeting apps offer accessible learning resources.

Consider gradually giving your children more financial responsibility through modern tools: a debit card with spending notifications, shared access to family subscription services to understand ongoing costs, or contributing to household expenses via payment-sharing apps. This helps build practical skills and emotional readiness for financial independence.

Equally important is teaching them to recognise when they're in over their head financially. Help them understand the difference between everyday money stress and serious financial trouble. Make sure they can access financial counselling services or trusted adults when needed.

Essential Skills

Today's readiness spans digital safety, health self-advocacy, mental well-being, access to transport, car maintenance, administrative and consumer rights, home care, and the networks that sustain them.

Young adults require digital responsibility: safeguarding themselves from online fraud, understanding privacy laws, setting up accounts across different platforms, recognising romance and employment scams, and managing their digital footprint. Consumer protection agencies report that sophisticated online scams increasingly target young adults. However, digital literacy alone isn't sufficient; they also need the confidence to trust their instincts when something feels off and the communication skills to verify suspicious requests.

Health management skills now include navigating telehealth appointments, using prescription delivery services, understanding mental health support apps, and knowing when digital solutions aren't enough. Recent global events have normalised many digital health services, making these skills essential rather than optional. However, the most important skill is learning to advocate for oneself in healthcare settings, such as clearly describing symptoms, asking questions when unsure, and persisting when feeling unheard. Many young adults find it difficult to transition from paediatric care, where parents facilitated communication, to adult healthcare, where they must speak for themselves.

Help them understand the difference between everyday adjustment stress, the overwhelm of new responsibilities, occasional loneliness, or academic pressure, and more serious mental health concerns that require professional attention. They should know how to access counselling services, recognise the signs when they need support, and understand that seeking help shows strength rather than weakness.

Transport and logistics knowledge reflects modern realities: safely using rideshare services, understanding sustainable transport options, managing digital check-ins and QR codes, and navigating travel through transport apps. But practical skills are also important: handling insurance, basic car maintenance, knowing what to do when public transport fails, and staying safe in unfamiliar areas.

Basic administration involves managing digital rental applications, understanding online bill payments, navigating government websites through official portals, and recognising legitimate versus fraudulent messages. Since most government transactions now happen online, these skills are essential for independent living. They also need to know their rights and responsibilities as tenants, employees, and consumers, along with knowledge that protects them from exploitation and helps them handle disputes confidently.

Home management goes beyond cooking basics; it includes understanding how utilities operate, knowing when to call professionals instead of attempting repairs, handling common issues like blocked drains or pest infestations, and creating a healthy living environment. These practical skills help prevent minor problems from turning into costly emergencies.

Perhaps most importantly, young adults must learn to independently build and sustain support networks. This involves forming friendships without parental assistance, maintaining relationships over distances, and developing professional networks that can foster career advancement. They require confidence in social settings, the skill to converse with strangers, and the emotional intelligence to nurture relationships over time.

Preparation becomes even more vital for families facing complex situations. Single parents need to be more systematic in addressing all aspects. Conversely, parents dealing with strained relationships might concentrate on practical steps to show care when emotional discussions are difficult.

The aim isn't to remove all life challenges but to foster confidence and the skills that help young adults handle modern independence with resilience. Each skill learned while support is available serves as a base for confident decision-making when they're on their own. More importantly, they learn to recognise when they need assistance and how to seek it properly. This is the most vital life skill of all.

Teaching life skills prepares our children for the workplace and also gets us ready. Each time we allow them to take responsibility, we practice managing our independence from them. Watching them cook, handle banking, or book appointments shows us they can manage, and this reassurance makes farewelling less frightening. The goal isn't perfection but confidence, built slowly so neither parent nor child feels overwhelmed. In this way, nurturing independence at home also nurtures the heart: every skill shared helps parents shift from being managers to supporters, easing the transition for both.

Most parents find that practical readiness is the rehearsal, while emotional readiness is the performance. And unlike your child's departure, you can't practice being ready for it. You can only build the strength to survive if you are unprepared.

Preparing the Heart

Creating Support Structures

The ideal time to build support networks into your life is not when the house falls silent, but while it is still lively and noisy. When children leave home, the relationship that often becomes more central is with your partner or yourself. For couples, this is a great opportunity to rediscover shared interests beyond family logistics: dinners without interruptions, going for walks together, or planning a trip unrelated to the school calendar. For single parents, preparation might involve strengthening bonds with siblings, parents, or close friends who can offer emotional support when the house is quieter. These relationships become anchors.

Conversations about what lies ahead, hopes for the future, and fears about the transition foster resilience. In a world where mental health is more openly discussed, couples counselling or coaching is increasingly normalised as a way of preparing for this shift. Whatever the form, nurturing these relationships ensures that when parenting is no longer the central focus, love and connection remain plentiful.

Friendships, community bonds, and even professional connections can ease the landing when children leave home. Too often, parents, especially mothers, realise too late that their social world has shrunk around their caregiving role. Reconnecting with old friends, nurturing neglected relationships, or joining community groups while children are still at home provides a ready-made support network when the transition occurs. For single parents, this preparation is not optional but essential; when the child has been the primary daily companion, the absence can feel especially keen.

Building networks early fosters companionship and a sense of continuity.

Building Emotional Skills

Every small separation serves as practice for the bigger goodbye. School camps, overnight stays with friends, or a child's first independent holiday give parents chances to consider their feelings and learn how to manage them. These moments prompt reflection: What makes you most anxious? What helps you find your rhythm again? What habits, like journaling, exercise, or meditation, help you stay grounded when they are away? Today, mindfulness apps, breathing exercises, and even digital therapy sessions offer practical tools for emotional regulation. Developing these habits before the big departure makes the transition easier. By viewing these minor separations as rehearsal, parents start to see that conflicts exist together and that resilience develops not in the absence of discomfort but through practising how to handle it.

Creating New Rhythms

Preparation is also practical. Parents who begin exploring new activities while their children are still at home establish a natural rhythm after they leave. Whether joining a new club, trying an art class, or engaging in nature-based activities, these pursuits remind both parent and child that life is expanding. Today's opportunities are endless: online courses, volunteering platforms, and digital groups allow people to grow from home while staying connected. Some parents also use this stage to update budgets, seek advice from financial planners, or adjust routines. These small yet meaningful actions show that independence is something everyone in the family can have. Developing new rhythms and making new plans helps children see that their parents' lives are full and rewarding, easing their guilt about leaving.

Building support networks, rehearsing emotional responses, and creating a new life for yourself before children leave home deserve much deeper exploration after they're gone. The chapters ahead continue these themes.

The Slow Goodbye

When children leave home, parents face a deep emotional challenge that goes well beyond their physical absence. The worry doesn't stop when the door closes behind them; it can grow when you can no longer see that they're safe, fed, and coping with everyday life.

Most departures are not just one-off events but subtle signs that unfold over months or even years. The laundry pile diminishes. Fewer plates are used at dinner. A shared phone tracker is turned off. One mother perfectly captured this slow transition. She explained that her daughter stopped sharing her location on Find My iPhone. She realised then that the chapter was closing. It wasn't a cruel or deliberate act, just a simple boundary being set. Each moment hints that the chapter is coming to an end. For parents, these signs can cut deep.

When the rooms are empty, the mind is seldom at rest. Parents often lie awake wondering if their child is eating properly, paying their bills on time, or navigating relationships safely. The instinct to protect doesn't diminish just because the nest is quiet. One mother described how her son still rang during the week in his first semester away from home, despite their Sunday call agreement. Another father chuckled as he recalled his daughter asking for "no daily texts," only to message him three times a day in the first month. These stories demonstrate how parents and children need to adapt to new rhythms of contact, often in surprising ways.

Behind this adjustment lie deeper questions: Will we stay close? Do they still need us? Will they turn to us when life gets tough?[2] These are not just irrational fears. They reflect the real challenge of shifting from protector to supporter while maintaining a meaningful connection. Each act of independence, whether paying their own bills or managing travel alone, can be seen as an opportunity to celebrate growth rather than mourn loss. Learning to balance worry with trust becomes one of the key emotional tasks of this stage. A relationship built with care can withstand this change.

Recognising the gradual nature of goodbye softens the shock when the final moment of departure arrives. It helps parents understand that worry, while natural, can coexist with pride in their child's growing independence.

Abrupt Departures

Not every child's departure happens gradually. Sometimes, the departure comes suddenly, driven by conflict, opportunity, or unresolved tension, and the feeling can be as if the floor has dropped out. Unlike slow goodbyes that allow parents to prepare emotionally, sudden departures leave them in shock, often with unfinished conversations, unspoken apologies, or relationships hanging in the air.

One mother, whose daughter left after a heated argument, described the silence that followed as a wound. In the following months, she started writing letters, never knowing if they were read. The ritual became a way of holding space, keeping connection alive even in silence. Almost a year later, a short text arrived, unexpected and small but enough to signal that the door had not closed completely.

When departures happen suddenly, healing often takes uneven steps rather than smooth progressions. Some parents find professional counselling or mediation helpful, creating a safe space to untangle conflicts that caused the departure. Others turn to peer support through local groups or online forums, where stories of reconciliation remind them that distance doesn't always mean finality. Small gestures become meaningful during these times: sending a birthday card, posting a photo of a shared tradition, or sending a simple message on a special day. These acts of presence, given without pressure or expectation, weave threads of continuity that can withstand even difficult separations.

Sudden departures test patience and resilience in ways that planned transitions rarely do. However, they also teach parents about persistence. Staying open without forcing closeness and trusting that even fragile threads can eventually reconnect into something more substantial is vital.

Complex Circumstances

Beyond timing, some empty nest transitions are driven by circumstances that challenge usual ideas of readiness and celebration. A child's departure might be linked to financial hardship, custody disputes, family breakdown, or external pressures that force the issue before anyone feels prepared. For these families, leaving is less about reaching milestones and more about necessity: a scholarship that can't be refused, a job opportunity that won't wait, or household instability that makes staying less safe.

Ellie understood the scholarship was a blessing. Her son had worked hard for it, and the chance to study interstate with all expenses covered was something she could never have managed alone. Yet, as a single mother, he was her dependent, her dinner companion, the one who helped her make sense of the day's challenges, and her reason for cooking a proper meal. When he left at eighteen, she felt the loss twice over. The house didn't just lose a child; it lost its heartbeat. The celebration everyone anticipated felt hollow. She was truly proud, yet quietly devastated, and no one seemed to understand that both could be true at the same time.

These transitions do not follow simple emotional stories. Instead, they involve practical and relationship challenges that must be handled at the same time. As a single parent, you might feel the loss more strongly because your child was not just someone you relied on but also a constant companion and partner in life's struggles. Divorced parents may find it difficult to manage different household rules and expectations. Even in stable families, financial pressures, health issues, or other crises can speed up separation, leaving you emotionally overwhelmed while trying to deal with the practical side of things.

For parents facing complex circumstances, resilience comes from finding strategies tailored to their unique situation rather than using a one-size-fits-all approach. Equally vital is recognising sources of support beyond the immediate family: friends who understand the issue, community groups that provide practical assistance, or professional counsellors who can offer perspective during chaotic times. These external supports don't eliminate the challenge but help parents avoid facing the difficulty alone.

Building Strength for What's Ahead

Preparation aims to build confidence that your work is nearly finished. Parents can't foresee every challenge, whether it's worry about their child's loneliness in a new city, unexpected financial issues, or their own waves of grief. However, emotional strength, practical readiness, and strong support systems mean departure doesn't entirely empty life. It isn't about bouncing back to what was, but about adapting meaningfully, reshaping the self while carrying love forward in new forms.

This preparation matters equally to children. They enter adulthood more easily when they know their parents are not floundering but thriving in parallel growth journeys. Independence feels lighter when shared with parents who have embraced their evolution rather than endured it.

Technology gives families new ways to stay connected despite the distance. Weekly video calls, family group chats, or shared playlists can strengthen relationships across continents. However, digital connection also introduces challenges that parents must learn to handle. Messages might go unanswered, not because of rejection but because of the busy routines everyone has. One father shared feeling upset when his son didn't reply to texts from London, only to realise later that silence meant he was busy, not emotionally distant. Social media adds another subtle layer. A kind comment on Instagram may sometimes embarrass a young adult rather than make them feel loved.

Learning the new rules of connection prepares the heart for modern parenthood. The screens that once distracted your teenagers from you now become the main way you reach them. Technology doesn't eliminate distance; it simply changes its form. It means stepping back when your instinct is to reach out, giving space when you want to close gaps, and allowing children to curate their own lives while remaining genuinely available when they invite you in. They haven't withdrawn from you. It's a sophisticated form of love that has adapted to changing needs.

What emerges from careful preparation is not a flawless departure but a clear one. You can't make this moment painless, but you can make it meaningful. Checklists build confidence, daily routines develop into new rhythms, and persistent worry gradually turns into earned trust. You have been developing two parallel types of readiness: theirs for independence, yours for a rich, purposeful life.

When the goodbye finally arrives, if you've prepared well, it hits differently: not painlessly, but meaningfully. You realise that all this preparation wasn't about getting them ready to leave you. It was about making you ready to let them go while staying true to who they need you to be: not their daily manager, but their constant anchor. The house may be empty, but the relationship isn't. It simply shifts from the rooms you share into the space you build together.

The next chapter examines that choice, that deliberate, ongoing act of creating connection. Just as we have prepared the home and the house for our children to leave, the next chapter focuses on evolving and what happens after they've gone (and sometimes come back).

Reflection and Practices

Individual Reflection Prompts

- What is one small daily change you've noticed that signals your child's growing independence? How does it make you feel?
- Think about your own parents. How did they experience children leaving? How do you want your story to be the same, or different?

Practical Awareness Activity

- The Checklists Exercise: Write two short lists: *Skills my child needs before leaving, and Supports I need as they go.*
- Compare them. Where do you see balance? Where do you see gaps?

Creative Journalling Exercise

- Imagine creating a ceremony or symbolic act for your child's departure. What does it include: objects, words, actions, blessings? How could you mark the shift for yourself as well as for them?

Key Takeaway

Preparation is not about avoiding the pain of letting them go but building emotional and practical resilience that both parent and child can step into the next stage with confidence, trust, and a sense of continuity.

Chapter 5

The Evolution of Home

Maggie was asking an AI app how to tell her 26-year-old to clean the bathroom when she realised how absurd her situation was. Eight months after her son, Tom, moved back home, she sought parenting advice about someone who manages a team of twelve at work but leaves wet towels on the bathroom floor. The empty nest she had carefully created, with her art supplies spread across the dining table and 6 am yoga sessions in the living room, had become a household of two adults who had forgotten how to live together.

Maggie believed she had already passed through this phase. The separation, the empty house, the final farewell. Now she wondered if she had ever truly grasped what it meant to find release. It's not a place, but a skill practised over and over, each time in a different way, with varying rules, until she realised the nest was never meant to remain empty. It was meant to stay adaptable.

Maggie's confusion highlights a wider cultural shift. The traditional view of childhood dependence giving way to complete adult independence is being replaced by more cyclical, adaptable patterns of connection and mutual support. While Chapter 4 concentrated on preparing the heart and the home, this chapter considers how the home changes after children leave and when they come back. It discusses the rise of the boomerang generation, where adult children return home after periods of independence. It traces how the empty nest became a cultural norm, looks at the forces now reversing it, and shows how modern Australian families are rethinking space, boundaries, and what it means to be a successful adult.

When Empty Nests Began to Fill Again

Maggie's experience with her son illustrates a trend reshaping Australian families. Just over half of young men (54%) and 47% of young women aged 18 to 29 continue living at home with their parents, and 13% of Australians, equivalent to 858,000 households, have had an adult child move back in within the past 12 months.[1] These figures go beyond housing; they show deep shifts in how families respond to economic and social changes. The COVID-19 pandemic made remote work normal, reducing the importance of location for employment. What started as emergency measures for many families became long-term lifestyle choices as both generations found unexpected advantages.

For Maggie, the change started two years earlier when Tom first left. While he was gone, she turned his gym into her art studio, with canvases replacing soccer posters and her easel taking the place of his desk. She had adapted to the suddenly too-big house, started enjoying being on her own, and built new routines around her creative pursuits. Then, the economics of living independently brought him back.

Tom carefully calculated his finances. He was paying $600

a week for a room in a Brisbane share house while trying to save for a house deposit. With remote work possible, moving back home meant he could save $30,000 a year and spend more time with his mum. His friends thought he was either broke or having a breakdown, but it felt like the first sensible financial decision he'd made in years.

Adult children may be weighing up the economic benefits of independent living against returning home, balancing financial practicality with social expectations of what independence should entail.

The Remaking of Space

Boomerang arrangements are most successful when parents and adult children establish clear boundaries and practical agreements, ideally short, simple, and written down.

Those who've transformed a child's space into something that suits their needs, like an office, exercise area, or creative sanctuary, may face what Maggie experienced. Packing up her studio felt like losing something she'd worked hard to create. But they couldn't pretend he was just visiting. This was his home again, which meant fundamental changes for both of them. The hardest lesson is philosophical rather than logistical: learning to hold space for two truths. This is still your home, and it's his home again. Neither claim cancels the other, but neither leaves you unchanged.

Establishing what could be called adult roommate rules becomes necessary: a returning child pays a fixed weekly amount for room and board, does their own laundry, and takes turns cooking dinner. Guidelines that weren't needed during teenage years also come up: no commenting on sleep schedules unless they affect household function, mutual respect for work-from-home space, and providing advance notice for overnight guests.

The negotiations show how much everyone has changed during the separation. Tom has developed different standards for household cleanliness and food choices, while Maggie has become more protective of her morning routines and personal space. In the first month, Maggie found herself trying to treat him like a visitor, which made her resentful and made him feel infantilised. They had awkward conversations about money, household responsibilities, and privacy.

Treating a returning child as a dependent teenager or a temporary guest creates tension. The key lies in finding a new dynamic that acknowledges everyone's growth during the separation.

Mental Health and Modern Adulthood

While financial pressures drive many boomerang returns, the phenomenon also reflects generational shifts in how young adults approach mental health and family relationships. Today's young adults are economically practical and emotionally literate in ways previous generations weren't permitted to be. They've been taught to name their struggles, seek support, and recognise that vulnerability isn't weakness. Now they're asking parents to live by those same principles. Generation Z reports closer relationships with parents than previous generations and a greater willingness to seek family support during psychological challenges.[2]

Emma, 24, moved back to her family's Adelaide farm after an anxiety-driven breakdown ended her graduate program in another state. She explained that although previous generations might have pushed through or suffered silently, she recognised she needed support, and her parents were willing to provide it. They gave her meaningful work on the farm.

An adult child might return for similar reasons; perhaps seeking emotional support during a mental health challenge, career transition, or life crisis. This reflects a generational shift from independence as the primary marker of successful adulthood to interdependence as a valued family principle. Adult children who return home aren't necessarily reliant; they are appreciated family members who contribute to household costs, assist with family duties, and lead active social lives.

This shift might challenge those raised with different values about self-reliance and asking for help. Maggie struggled with her own conditioning. She was raised to believe that needing to move back home meant failure. Learning to see Tom's decision as strategic rather than desperate required unlearning some deeply held beliefs about what independence and success actually mean.

These generational shifts in how young adults approach independence and support create new family dynamics. Yet while much attention is focused on how adult children navigate returning home, less is discussed about what this transition means for parents who are just beginning to rediscover themselves.

Midlife and the Housing Crunch

But here's what's rarely discussed: while adult children manage their own transitions, parents go through theirs as well. Boomerang arrangements shake up households and clash with the delicate new identities parents have been carefully building. They create a complex psychological landscape for parents facing their own midlife transitions, returning when you're starting to get your life back on track or believe it is on track.

Maggie felt this tension deeply. She'd finally started prioritising her health with regular exercise, better sleep, and time for meditation. When Tom came back, she fell into old habits of staying up late to chat with him, cooking elaborate meals, and managing household chores around his schedule. She had to be mindful to keep up the self-care routines she had built.

A returning child can disrupt carefully cultivated routines and self-care practices that took months or years to establish. Research on boomerang families shows mixed outcomes: some parents report renewed purpose, while others experience increased stress during midlife transitions. Some enjoy helping adult children navigate early career challenges. Others feel their needs are being postponed again, creating resentment that shadows what should be a supportive reunion.

The physical demands of renewed caregiving, such as later bedtimes, increased grocery shopping, and accommodating different schedules, can worsen midlife health challenges. However, many parents also feel energised by having family around during a life stage that can feel isolating.

The boomerang effect aligns with another demographic reality: ageing parents who may need to downsize or access aged care services. This generates a timing challenge where adult children need affordable housing just as parents face their own housing transitions. Maggie, now 58, is concerned about this overlap. Tom is saving for a house deposit, but she and her husband are also debating whether their four-bedroom home still makes sense as they age. The questions increase: Can they downsize while he's still there and help with the move? Should they wait until he moves out again? What if he doesn't go, or what if he does but they need help in their seventies? The timing of one generation's move coincides uncomfortably with another's downsizing, leading to conflicting housing needs within the same family.

You may encounter similar timing issues with your own housing plans while assisting your adult child's housing needs. Financial advisors are increasingly advising families to budget for the possibility of adult children returning home and to plan for retirement and potential care requirements. The old notion that children's financial independence happens during their peak earning years is no longer valid. Property developers are responding with purpose-built multigenerational housing that includes separate entrances, kitchenettes, and flexible living areas.[3] You might also find yourself improvising, such as turning your garage into a small studio, listing the spare room on Airbnb between stays, or trying out six-month house charters that set noise, guest, and financial norms. Mortgage brokers report rising numbers of three-generation applications, where grandparents, parents, and adult children buy together to secure housing across generations.

Global Context

The experience of boomerang arrangements varies greatly across different cultural backgrounds. Cultural differences happen within a global context where multigenerational living is becoming more common. In Italy and Spain, living at home until 30 has long been normal, while in the United States, the percentage of 25-34-year-olds living with their parents hit its highest level since the 1940s during the pandemic and has remained high.[4] In 2024, the OECD reported that 28% of young adults across member countries live with their parents, up from 21% in 2007. This indicates that Australia's experience reflects wider economic and social changes rather than local anomalies.[5]

What looks like failure through one cultural lens looks like resilience through another. The question isn't whether adult children should live at home; it's whether we can develop new cultural scripts that honour both generations' needs without shame. Ideas of adulthood and family life vary across cultures, but they all emphasise that independence alone cannot define success. If the model changes, the measure of success must change, too.

Redefining Success

The boomerang phenomenon forces a reconsideration of what fundamentally constitutes successful family development. The traditional, linear childhood dependence model has become a looped experience.

Tom reflects on how external perceptions don't always match reality. His friends who moved out at 18 and never returned aren't necessarily more successful. Some struggle with debt, loneliness, and career uncertainty. Living at home gave him financial stability, the ability to be selective about opportunities, and emotional support to take career risks he wouldn't have felt comfortable taking alone.

Adult children might be making similar calculations about success that focus on financial stability and emotional wellbeing instead of traditional marks of independence. This change calls for new ways to understand family progress. Rather than judging success by how quickly children become independent, it is now measured by relationship quality, mutual support through tough times, and collective resilience.

Maggie has gained a new perspective on her experience. She thought she had learned to let go when Tom first moved to university, but his return showed her that it isn't just a one-time event. It's an ongoing process of loving and supporting him while maintaining her own identity and boundaries. The journey has been more challenging than the initial empty nest phase, but more rewarding.

Navigating a child's return requires different skills than the initial letting go, but it also presents unexpected chances for deeper connection and personal growth that the first departure never offered.

The Future of Elastic Homes

The economic factors driving boomerang arrangements show no signs of easing. Climate change introduces new pressures through extreme weather events, rising energy costs, and potential displacement. Mental health awareness continues to grow, with young adults more inclined to seek family support during psychological challenges. Technology maintains family bonds across distances while also enabling location-independent work.

These trends indicate that multigenerational living

arrangements will become more common rather than just temporary disruptions.[6] This change impacts housing policy, urban planning, healthcare, and social services. It also calls for new research on how families can effectively manage flexible arrangements while maintaining personal growth and family bonds.

Once considered the final stage of development, the empty nest now appears as part of a more cyclical, responsive family narrative. The future of family isn't about emptiness but flexibility: homes that expand and contract with changing needs, relationships that deepen through renegotiation rather than distance, and definitions of success that prioritise adaptation over rigid independence.

As Maggie realised, the skills required for this new family model go far beyond the initial "letting go" that empty nest discussions usually focus on. The story of modern Australian families is one of constant adaptation, where the home becomes less a place to pass through and more a resource shared across generations and changing circumstances.

When rooms change, so does identity. Not back to mothering but forward into something more complex: a version of home where multiple adult identities coexist, negotiate, and adapt. You are still a parent but also a person with your own rhythms, needs, and boundaries. Learning to hold both without guilt is the task of this stage.

This negotiation occurs not only in households but also within bodies. Maggie observed that Tom's return stress coincided with worsening hot flushes, disrupted sleep, and midlife changes she had been managing, which intensified under the pressure of renegotiating home life. The empty nester generation often lines up with the menopause generation, and these transitions don't happen in isolation.

The next chapter explores how the empty nest intersects with menopause, shifting visibility, and the aging female body. It's about refusing to disappear and redefining beauty, presence, and worth on your own terms in a changing body, whether the world is ready.

Reflections and Practices

Individual Reflection Prompts

- What space in your home changed most when your child left, and what did it mean to you when it became yours? How did it feel to adjust it again when they returned?
- Think about your daily rhythms: meals, TV time, bedtimes. How have they shifted since your adult child returned? Which changes feel sustainable, and which feel draining?

Practical Awareness Activity – Boundary Mapping

- Draw a simple sketch of your home. Shade the shared spaces and those that feel like yours. If these spaces overlap, what conversations might help clarify expectations?
- List three "non-negotiables" you need for your well-being in a shared household (e.g. quiet in the evenings, privacy, financial contribution). Circle the one that matters most and write a sentence about how you might communicate it.

Creative Journalling Exercise – Reframing Success

- Write a short reflection: "Success in this season of family life looks like…" Don't define it by old cultural scripts (e.g. independence at all costs). Instead, write it about connection, balance, and growth that feels right for you.

Key Takeaway

Home is never static. The return of adult children can be disruptive and enriching, unsettling and connective. Families can transform the boomerang return into a season of deeper connection and resilience by clearly renegotiating space, roles, and expectations.

Chapter 6

Menopause and Visibility in the Empty Nest Years

She stood in front of the mirror. Her body, once home to children clinging to her hip, now stood alone. The reflection showed signs of ageing, many creases, wrinkles, softening skin, and silvery strands, yet it also raised a question: Who sees me anyway?

She exercises to stay fit and tries to dress well. She looks online for style tips and haircuts suitable for women over 60. She attends makeup classes and is thinking about vascular surgery for her prominent varicose veins. Still, she isn't overly worried about medical or surgical changes. Why should she be? Her body is ageing, and she accepts it. As her sense of visibility changed, so did she. Acceptance, she'd learned, was the radical act of refusing to wage war on her own flesh. It was choosing presence over perfection, inhabitation over apology.

She sometimes teased her daughters with visions of herself as a crazy old lady who would fling propriety to the wind. In truth, that imagined future was less a threat than a promise: a playful rebellion that lived alongside the discipline keeping her strong. The fire she carried was ignited by women who spoke truths society often tried to silence.

Now that your nest is empty, your body—once constantly claimed by children—has space to be rediscovered on your own terms. This chapter explores what happens when the empty nest coincides with menopause, changes in social visibility, and the complex process of ageing in a culture that has never truly understood what to do with women beyond their reproductive years. It addresses some of the key issues many women face when experiencing an empty nest, without claiming to cover them comprehensively. These are considerations, observations, and possibilities rather than definitive answers.

It's about the revolutionary act of refusing to fade away, redefining beauty through flesh and bone rather than ideals, and discovering that the body that has been a home to others for so long can finally be yours. We'll explore the realities of menopause and caregiving during midlife and consider how you can craft new stories about visibility and ageing. You're not becoming invisible; quite the opposite is happening.

The Physical Foundation of Feminist Awakening

The feminist voices before us have influenced countless women in midlife and beyond today, knowingly or unknowingly. The women who shaped our generation's understanding of bodily autonomy didn't speak in abstractions; they talked about periods, pregnancy, pleasure, and power.

When Germaine Greer wrote about female sexuality in The Female Eunuch, she discussed your right to fully inhabit your body. When Gloria Steinem spoke about reproductive choice, she rooted political arguments in physical reality. This embodied feminism permeated everyday life through conversations about birth control at kitchen tables, discussions of workplace discrimination while folding laundry, and late-night talks about marriage and motherhood that recognised the physical toll of caring for others. More than academic debates, they were body-based truths spoken woman to woman.

A new wave of Australian voices has taken up the baton, reshaping the conversation for women like us. Clementine Ford speaks openly about rage, motherhood, and autonomy. Yumi Stynes brings honesty and empathy to topics once considered taboo, like periods and menopause, helping us feel less alone with our physical changes. Broadcasters such as Narelda Jacobs and Jacinta Parsons ensure that stories of race, queerness, illness, and creativity are recognised as central to women's lives. These voices have laid a foundation that allows women to see midlife bodily changes as the next chapter in a lifelong conversation about physical autonomy.

The global chorus reaches all of us, weaving through our consciousness like a soundtrack to your transformation. Gloria Steinem embodies silver-haired defiance, Naomi Wolf exposes the damage of beauty myths, and Erica Jong redefines female desire beyond youth. The author bell hooks (who styled her name in lower case to shift focus from the individual to her ideas), Brené Brown, and Tarana Burke offer new languages of love, vulnerability, and truth-telling that help reshape how you see yourself and others. Thinkers and storytellers like Esther Perel, Mona Eltahawy, Alexandra Solomon, and Chimamanda Ngozi Adichie continue challenging cultural scripts, broadening our definitions of identity, intimacy, and self-respect.

These voices, past and present, local and global, offered more than ideas. They teach you something revolutionary: that your body isn't a problem to solve but a story to honour, that the physical changes you're experiencing aren't failures but chapters: messy, uncomfortable, and yours to write. They provide the language, tools, and permission to claim space, live more visibly, and start again on your own terms.

Once distant or radical, feminism now appears in the mirror beside you as you adjust your hair, clothes, or posture. It has become personal, embodied, and undeniable. Feminist legacies matter because they influence how you face the empty nest years, menopause, and shifting visibility.

Midlife Transitions

Midlife coincides with a profound sensation of slipping into invisibility. Yet the absence of daily parenting also creates an unexpected freedom: you can choose how to inhabit this new visibility, unburdened by the constant demands of the household. While mirrors still reflect you, sometimes, the world does not. Yet understanding the physical realities of this life stage, from hormonal shifts to caregiving demands, can transform what feels like loss into opportunity.

Menopause, caring for ageing parents, shifts in identity, and mental health changes often overlap, increasing both emotional strain and the potential for deep personal growth. Midlife transitions don't occur in isolation or impact all women equally. Rural, First Nations, and migrant women often face additional obstacles when accessing healthcare, mental health support, or social services, particularly for menopause management and elder care. Geography, culture, and socioeconomic factors add further complexity to an already multifaceted experience, creating diverse pathways through what might seem like a universal life stage.

Physical changes often reflect emotional upheaval, yet reclaiming one's body can foster a more profound sense of acceptance. Recognising this relationship provides the foundation for exploring the major physical transition many women encounter at this stage.

Menopause: Your Body's Revolution

Menopause manifests through your body: hot flushes that wake you at 3 am, joints that ache in new spots, and skin that reacts differently to touch. At the same time, your empty house can provide breathing room to notice and attend to these symptoms, which are no longer pushed aside by children's schedules.

In rural areas, the physical isolation compounds the bodily challenges. Women living hours from specialised care often endure symptoms in silence.[1] One mother, 90 kilometres from the nearest GP, described the additional burden: *The drive to town made my back ache worse, and I never knew if the doctor would take my symptoms seriously anyway.*

According to Jean Hailes for Women's Health, 83% of Australian women experience noticeable menopausal symptoms, but only 21% feel they have sufficient support to manage them.[2] Behind these figures are women like Jane, a Melbourne mum whose body seemed to rebel just as her nest emptied. *I'd wake up soaked in sweat, feeling like my body was betraying me right when I thought I might get it back.*

Your physical symptoms might mirror the emotional

upheaval: brain fog that makes you question your competence, mood swings that feel foreign in your own skin, changes in sexual response that alter how you relate to your body's capacity for pleasure. A 2024 Women's Agenda report found that 60% of Australian women experience mood swings during menopause. These are physical sensations of anxiety, rage, or sadness that seem to emanate from the cellular level.[3]

Jane found relief through workshops at Jean Hailes and yoga classes that helped her reconnect with her changing body. *Yoga didn't stop the hot flushes, although they taught me that my body was strong and capable. I learned to breathe through the changes instead of fighting them.* She also realised that, ironically, her children's departure gave her the mental space to put her body's needs first for the first time in decades. The cruel irony: just as you reclaim your body from motherhood, menopause reclaims it from predictability. But unlike motherhood, which demands that you serve others, menopause demands that you only listen to yourself. Your body is completing one of nature's most profound transitions. But without support, you can feel abandoned by the very flesh that carried you through decades of life.

Naomi Wolf once wrote, *Ageing in women is not 'our fault', but we are made to feel that way.*[4] This insight illuminates why midlife hormonal shifts are not only medical events but social ones, laden with cultural expectation and shame. Naming and supporting menopause, while it is effective health advocacy, is also a feminist action. It is your reclaiming of bodily autonomy that those earlier voices fought to establish.

However, bodies rarely complete one cycle before the next

begins. Just as you're recognising the signs of menopause—hot flushes, brain fog, and mood swings—another set of physical challenges arises, this time from the generation who raised you.

The Caregiving Body: Strength and Strain

When the daily physical demands of raising children lessen, you might find your body called back into action, this time to care for ageing parents. The empty nest sharpens this change: with children grown, the caregiving role often shifts to ageing parents, turning the newfound physical space of the home into a different kind of responsibility. The irony is clear: the body that finally felt free is suddenly lifting, supporting, and advocating again.

The physical demands are immediate and relentless. Sandra, managing her mother's dementia while navigating her own empty nest, described the toll: *My back hurt constantly from helping Mum transfer from bed to chair. My hands were dry and cracked from all the handwashing. My body felt like it was ageing faster than hers.* The 2025 Australian Seniors: Sandwich Generation Report reveals that women often make up two-thirds of carers while managing menopausal symptoms.[5] The convergence of physical symptoms you might experience, like hot flushes while lifting a parent, joint pain while managing medications, fatigue from interrupted sleep while providing emotional support, creates a compounding effect on your body.

But within this physical challenge, you might uncover unexpected strength. Linda discovered that the same yoga practice that aided with menopause also supported her caregiving stamina. *I learned to lift using my legs, not my back. I started taking five-minute breathing breaks between care tasks. My body became more deliberate, more aware.* The statistics are sobering: 9 in 10 carers experience burnout, and 65% worry about long-term health consequences.[6] When you learn to advocate for your physical needs, such as rest, medical care, and proper support equipment, you often find that this advocacy unexpectedly extends to your parents and yourself. Your body, stretched between caring for others and caring for yourself, becomes a teacher in recognising limits, setting boundaries, and understanding that physical sustainability requires active attention.

When The Body Becomes Invisible: The Cultural Gaze

The same society that once valued you primarily for your reproductive and nurturing capacity now seems to look right through you as those functions fade. This isn't a coincidence but rather the logical extension of a culture that has never learned to value women beyond their service to others.

The numbers reflect this lived experience: a 2024 Women's Agenda survey found that over 60% of Australian women aged 45-65 felt they were treated as less visible in public, professional, and social contexts.[7] This perceived fading isn't a reflection of your diminished worth but of deeply entrenched societal conditioning that equates female value with youth and reproductive potential.

The contrast is clear and intentional: midlife men are called distinguished, seasoned, or experienced. At the same time, women of the same age tend to be labelled past their prime or ignored altogether. In mainstream media and advertising, older women's bodies are either unseen or shown mainly in medical settings; problems to fix rather than lives being enjoyed.[8]

Rita from Esperance, Western Australia, said, *I didn't stop being beautiful. I just stopped being noticed. After a while, I started to believe that meant the same thing.* Her words capture how external invisibility can turn into internal self-doubt, creating a cycle where cultural neglect leads to self-diminishment. The phone calls, the busy dinners, and the lively interruptions are gone, leaving you more aware of how society overlooks you.

This is precisely the sort of story Erica Jong challenged in Fear of Flying, opposing the idea that women must choose between sensuality and independence. Her lively, daring, and intellectually courageous voice still rings true, reminding you that women in midlife aren't vanishing; they're being overlooked by a culture that hasn't yet learned to see them clearly.

Such cultural invisibility creates a strange feedback loop. You might start to move cautiously through space, dress conservatively, or speak more softly, not because your body needs to, but because the culture has taught you that your physical presence no longer counts. Your body internalises social neglect, turning cultural dismissal into personal diminishment.

Understanding this erasure as culturally constructed rather than naturally inevitable opens space for something radical: your choice to inhabit your body visibly, deliberately, and on your own terms. Yet out of this neglect, new movements of resistance are rising.

The Rise of Pro-Ageing

The term "anti-ageing" is beginning to sound not only outdated but also offensive. Where revolutions once took place in the streets or boardrooms, now it's happening in bathrooms, where you look in mirrors and choose to see strength instead of failure. At this point, your beauty becomes inherently political because it challenges the cultural idea that ageing bodies should apologise for simply existing.

Your soft belly tells stories of life carried and meals shared. Your veined hands reveal decades of work, love, and supporting others. Your stretch marks serve as maps of growth. Even your slowing gait is a rhythm earned, not a flaw to fix. Each mark proves a life fully lived, rather than a failure to stay young. These are reminders of motherhood past and your freedom to redefine beauty once the nest is quiet. In that quiet, you often find the courage to use red lipstick, wear colour unapologetically and statement earrings, and wear rebellion in your smile and reclaim the mirror for yourself.

Major beauty campaigns are slowly beginning to reflect this change. L'Oréal's Age Perfect features women whose beauty is rooted in their life experience, not just youthfulness.[9] However, this clever marketing still encourages women to spend money on enhancing their appearance. Australian style icons like Jenny Kee continue to prove that bold colours and creative expression don't fade with age. Instead, they often become more genuine and more authentic to themselves.

The most powerful transformations happen in your everyday moments: choosing bright lipstick for no special occasion, wearing a dress that shows your arms, and posting an unfiltered photo. You are not being vain. These are declarations that your body still deserves celebration. One woman from the South Coast shared that she started wearing lipstick again, not because she was going out, but because she liked how it felt against her lips when she smiled. Her body remembered pleasure.

Mona Eltahawy suggests that the most subversive thing a woman can do is live out loud.[10] In your midlife, beauty becomes inherently political in its refusal to shrink, apologise, or vanish. Reclaiming visibility isn't just about how others perceive you; it's about how you choose to inhabit your body. Beauty is only one part of the story; embodiment furthers your reclamation into daily rituals and lived experience.

Your Body as Home

This stage fosters a new relationship with your body, not as an ornament to be admired from afar or displayed, but as a vessel for your experience and joy. Your body was meant to be inhabited from within: felt, lived, and moved through space with authority earned from decades of survival, service, and finally, self-recognition. Reclaiming your body might involve ocean swims that wash away years of self-consciousness, forest walks that reconnect you to natural rhythms, Pilates that builds strength from within, or joining an over-50s dance troupe where laughter is more important than perfection.

Rituals, while small, can be life-changing: a quiet bath lit by candlelight becomes a self-care meditation, a slow stretch to morning birdsong becomes a joy, or investing in soft linen sheets because your body deserves comfort after decades of service. They are acts of presence. They say: I am still here. I still matter.

You might rediscover sensuality not through performance for others, but through touch, warmth, and pleasure that is self-directed. Your hand resting on a sun-warmed shoulder becomes an act of self-compassion. The satisfaction of your strong legs carrying you up a hill symbolises capability. Wearing silk pyjamas for the first time in decades, not for anyone else's benefit, but simply because your skin deserves kindness after years of rough practicality.

Physical changes happen; your skin loosens, hair grows whiter, and curves settle into new shapes. No longer bound by the anxious gaze of youth or the exhausting pressure of comparison, you might feel more authentic than ever. Your pleasure becomes simpler, slower, and more conscious, like settling into the rhythm of your breath.

Physical intimacy might evolve, too. With no children in the house, you and your partner might rediscover intimacy in simple, unhurried ways: touch and laughter return without the fear of interruption. Without the urgency of reproductive concerns or the exhaustion of active parenting, your touch can become more conscious. Sharing morning coffee becomes as intimate as passion once was, both expressions of bodies choosing connection rather than obligation. Increasing self-connection lays the groundwork for a novel type of visibility, deliberately chosen rather than randomly given. It becomes the foundation for something revolutionary: your decision to be seen on your own terms.

Visibility by Design

Your journey through menopausal change, caregiving stress, and cultural neglect brings you to this realisation: your body was never meant to vanish. Invisibility is a cultural construction that benefits those who profit from women's silence, rather than an inevitable result of ageing.

Your visibility is no longer about waiting to be noticed. It's about inhabiting your body with intention, wearing bold jewellery that catches light when you gesture, walking with the confidence of someone who has earned every line and curve, and taking up physical space without apology. It's about spreading your arms wide in conversation, sitting with legs uncrossed, laughing without covering your mouth. This is what terrifies patriarchy most: not women who rage against aging, but women who refuse to pretend it diminishes them. Women whose bodies carry history like armour, not shame.

When you choose to be seen, you're making a personal statement, but you're also showing younger women what 50, 60, 70 looks like when it refuses to apologise for existing. Your body becomes both the site of resistance and the method of revolution. Every time you move confidently through space, wear what brings you joy, or speak with the authority earned through decades of experience, you're rewriting the script that says older women's bodies should be grateful for whatever attention they receive.

Here's what the culture of bodily invisibility doesn't want you to know: you are at your most dangerous when your body stops seeking approval. You are most powerful when you realise you have nothing left to lose by inhabiting your physical self exactly as you are. Your body isn't a consolation prize for lost youth. Instead, it's evidence of a fully lived life. The hot flushes, the caregiving exhaustion, and the cultural dismissal taught your body to recognise its own resilience.

Your physical presence is not diminished by time; it's concentrated by experience.

When you choose to be visible, you show that life after intensive caregiving is about living more fully as yourself. Each time you speak up, take on something new, or refuse to step back, you challenge the belief that women should grow smaller with age. Power over decline emerges. You were never meant to disappear, and your perspective, steadiness, and strength are needed now more than ever. Younger women, too, need to see that a visible life continues well beyond motherhood, and a culture that once expected silence must face women who refuse to be set aside. For your adult children watching from a distance, let them see a mother still living fully, allowing them to imagine their own ageing differently.

This is your time: direct, purposeful, and entirely your own.

A Body, Still Yours

Your body remembers what your mind tries to minimise. It carries every embrace, every sleepless night, every moment of holding others up. It also remembers the feminist voices that insisted bodies matter, the moments of physical pleasure reclaimed, and the recognition that worth was never tied to youth or service to others.

Through menopause, cultural invisibility, and beauty that no longer seeks external validation, you emerge not despite but because of your body's changes. Your body remembers, and in that memory lies the foundation for everything that comes next. You also emerge because your nest is finally empty, and your home, like your body, can now be yours to inhabit fully.

In the next chapter, we explore what fills the spaces left in their absence. Having reclaimed your body as your own, you must now reckon with these spaces. Loneliness examines the often unspoken weight that arises when life slows, and the stillness feels heavy. It reminds us that while painful, it can also become a critical doorway to something you might not have expected.

Reflections and Practices

Individual Reflection Prompts

- When you look in the mirror today, what is one feature or mark on your body that tells a story? Write about the story it carries.
- What does "visibility" mean to you now? Write about a time you felt unseen, and how you want to choose to be seen differently.

Creative Journalling / Embodiment Exercises

- The Mirror Exercise
  Stand in front of the mirror. Instead of noticing what you want to change, name three things your body has carried you through. Write them down as a list of gratitude.
- Movement as Memory
  Choose a straightforward movement (stretching, dancing, walking) and write afterwards: *My body felt…* Notice not just pain or fatigue, but also strength, rhythm, or joy.

Future Visioning Prompt
- Write a declaration: *I refuse to disappear* because...
  Let it flow without editing. Make it bold, even defiant.

Key Takeaway

Your body carries memory, resilience, and beauty on its own terms. Midlife is not disappearance but emergence, a conscious choice to be visible, embodied, rebellious and unapologetically yourself.

PART III:

CHALLENGES AND OPPORTUNITIES

Chapter 7

Loneliness

Birthdays and Mother's Day were the worst. She bought herself champagne and flowers. Everyone else was busy. May was seeding time; farmers planted the grain at the start of winter. They worked day and night to make the most of the ground moisture after a heavy rain.

She had some friends, a supportive family, and a busy life. Yet loneliness crept in, catching her by surprise with its depth. The familiar school circles faded; the conversations dried up. Her nest had emptied before others' around her, and she stood apart, watching life go on. All around her, everything seemed to be shifting: her daughters gone, her parents ageing, her body changing, retirement looming. Surrounded by people, she still longed for someone who truly understood the drift from her old life, the loss of all she once was. She was lonely, but she didn't voice it aloud. Who admits to feeling lonely when everyone else seems part of a friendship group? She was at a loss as to who to call and wondered if anyone would notice if she disappeared.

The shame of loneliness lies in its cruelty. It whispers that good mothers should be selfless enough to feel only joy at their children's independence, that modern women should be complete enough not to need the daily rhythms of family life. But loneliness doesn't ask for your ideas about what you should feel; it simply appears. Naming it instead of hiding it begins to loosen its grip.

Loneliness is the absence of being known. And when the person who knew you best was the role you played rather than the woman you are, the empty nest doesn't just remove your children. It removes your witness.

Understanding the Landscape

It isn't a weakness or a social shortcoming, and it isn't one single feeling, either. Loneliness is a bridge, uncomfortable to cross and impossible to avoid, connecting who you were to who you're becoming. Understanding its architecture helps you walk across it rather than getting stuck halfway.

Social loneliness arises from the lack of daily interactions: casual chats at school events, spontaneous coffees with mates, or familiar faces at local gatherings that once built your sense of community. It's the hollow echo in spaces that used to buzz with social energy. Gayle, whose youngest son has started university, described it as suddenly realising all her friends were actually my son's friends' parents, without a thing left to say to each other.

Emotional loneliness runs deeper. It is characterised by the absence of a close bond with someone whose presence once brought you comfort, stability, or understanding. This often shows up as missing the emotional closeness of being needed, trusted, and confided in by your children. One mother shared that she wanted to text her daughter about her day, but remembered she has her own life now. She acknowledged that her daughter doesn't need to know about things she thought were funny, or that she saw her old teacher at the shops.

Existential loneliness burrows deep into your core. It is an unsettling feeling that your sense of self or purpose has diminished, and your role in the world no longer feels clear or appreciated. It arises from feeling fundamentally cut off from meaning itself. This loneliness questions, *'Who am I if I'm not needed in the same way?'*

Naming these distinctions doesn't erase the feeling but provides a map. Language becomes a lifeline, transforming what once seemed like a formless void. Research confirms what many women experience silently: one in three Australian women often feels lonely, despite having digital connections and busy social lives.[1] The paradox remains; people can surround you, yet you can still feel very lonely.

Recognising that others share this experience can be your first step away from the isolation caused by shame. Alongside these personal experiences, loneliness develops within cultural contexts that shape what family and separation mean.

When Culture Becomes Another Country

For some women, loneliness also carries the weight of cultural difference. Cultural loneliness is the feeling of being cut off when your culture and surroundings give you mixed messages about what family should be, how separation should happen, and how mothers are expected to feel when children leave. It can feel like being surrounded by people yet having no one who truly understands your experience, whether in your words or the unspoken values you carry.

Leila wouldn't have called herself lonely, not in the usual way. She had neighbours who waved, friends at community events, and a packed calendar. But something more profound changed when her daughter moved out. Amira's leaving didn't just empty the house; it created a quiet that Leila couldn't describe.

She made enough biryani to serve plates for a family that was no longer there. In Lebanon, homes were lively, noisy, and closely connected. In Sydney, independence was celebrated. Amira called it growing up. Leila called it fading away. She was proud, and Amira was thriving. But each night, as she packed away untouched leftovers, Leila felt grief. She missed the rhythms of their shared life: Friday dinners, aunties dropping by, and children running around. A friend once asked why she let her go. *That wasn't the hard part. The hard part was letting her go alone.*

Leila wasn't lacking people. She was lacking a connection that felt mutual, cultural, and alive. What made it worse was pretending she was fine. In public, she smiled, shared photos, and answered politely. In private, she sat at the table long after she had eaten, feeling the tension between the image of happiness and the experience of private sorrow.

Like Leila, you might discover that your loneliness isn't due to a lack of people but a lack of shared understanding. When no one recognises the significance of your loss, and when your grief is met with congratulations, isolation deepens and becomes more complex. What Leila experienced in silence reflects the lives of many others. Six months after Amira moved out, Leila began hosting Friday dinners again, not for family, but for other Lebanese mothers whose children had left home. They cooked together, ate together, and spoke Arabic around the table. The house was filled with noise again, different noises, meaningful noises. Leila was still lonely at times, but she wasn't alone. She had built community from absence.

Often, the loss of role and the breakdown of connection occur together, leaving many women surprised by how deep their loneliness can be.

When Role and Connection Disappear Together

The loneliness that follows the empty nest often carries a double burden: the loss of the mother role that once defined your daily purpose, and the simultaneous erosion of the social connections that came with that role. Research reveals what many discover with uncomfortable clarity: 35% of empty nesters report feeling lonely despite having full and active lives.[2] You might find that your friendships have been built around shared parenting experiences rather than deeper personal connections.

This realisation might be a shock and shame: dedicating yourself entirely to family life has allowed your independent social ties to fade. Rather than casting judgment, it's often a natural consequence of the intense demands of active parenting. When the scaffolding of family life is removed, your foundation of adult friendship may feel surprisingly fragile. The absence of a partner can intensify this experience, but even in a relationship, you might find that your social connections mainly revolve around your mothering role. When that role shifts, you must rebuild your daily routine and your entire social identity.

Landscapes of Loneliness

Loneliness wears different masks depending on where you live, but it speaks the same language of disconnection across all landscapes.

Rural: Distance

In rural areas, loneliness often has a practical dimension that compounds the emotional experience. Physical distance between neighbours, limited public transport, and fewer community gathering spaces can turn social connection into a significant effort requiring planning and energy.

Yvonne lived on a cattle property three hours from the nearest town. When her three sons were home, the drive to sporting events and school functions provided natural chances for chats with other parents; shared complaints about children's behaviour, quick coffees after parent meetings, and car-pooling arrangements that built friendships. She enjoyed the car rides to football matches, which were her social lifeline. She appreciated the company of all the mothers squeezed in, talking about everything but football. Now, those drives were alone, and the motivation to make the trip alone for social reasons felt harder to summon. The isolation was both geographic and social, without the usual meeting points children's activities used to offer; maintaining friendships needed deliberate effort that felt overwhelming when she was already enduring loss.

If you live in a rural area, you might describe this kind of loneliness: surrounded by vast open space that mirrors the emptiness you feel. *I can see for miles in every direction*, one mother shared, *but there's no one to see*. The same landscape that once felt peaceful and grounding can become a reflection of isolation. Research suggests that geographic isolation worsens emotional loneliness, with rural empty nesters reporting higher levels of social isolation than their urban counterparts.[3]

For many rural women, small changes become vital. Technology shifts from a convenience to a crucial link; video calls turn into scheduled lifelines, not just luxuries. You might find yourself scheduling social activities around farming seasons, opting for trips to town or courses during quieter times. Mobile services, from libraries to workshops, offer practical benefits and human connection. Regional women's groups provide understanding that crosses geographic boundaries, while purposeful town trips incorporate social aspects into essential journeys.

Urban: Proximity Without Intimacy
If distance determines rural loneliness, then in cities, the opposite can be just as harsh: closeness without real connection. Crowded streets, bustling cafes, and apartment living give the appearance of community but often only offer shallow interactions. Group chats hum with activity but lack genuine depth. Social media feeds portray active social lives yet hide the reality of lonely nights.

You can feel invisible in a city, surrounded by people but unnoticed, part of the crowd but not part of the community. The fast pace of city life can make genuine connections feel like a luxury. Jenny, a single mother whose daughter moved to another state for university, found herself eating dinner alone in restaurants to be around other people. *I'd sit there pretending to read, but really I was listening to other people's conversations, hungry for human voices that weren't coming from the television.* Her experience shows that loneliness is not confined to paddocks and long drives; it can thrive just as easily in crowded train stations and busy city streets, where invisibility becomes its own kind of isolation.

Digital Connection: Promise and Limitation

Technology now offers tools for connection across any distance. Video calls with distant children can bring genuine comfort, the sight of a familiar face lighting up the screen. Yet those same calls can also sharpen the reminder of absence, closing the gap for a moment only to widen it again when the conversation ends.

Online support groups and forums offer spaces where people can share their stories and be met with empathy. However, the absence of physical presence can make these bonds feel weaker, missing the warmth of a hand on yours or the comfort of sitting side by side. Social media promises community, but more often it draws you into comparison. Carefully curated feeds might leave you comparing your life to highlight reels of others, performing rather than connecting. Scrolling late at night may provide some comfort, yet it often leaves you feeling more isolated, staring at a screen instead of being part of the flow of your life.

The key is not to abandon digital spaces but to use them intentionally, as a bridge for meaningful interaction rather than a substitute for it (more on this shortly). Whether in rural or urban settings, online or offline, these experiences reveal a deeper truth: loneliness isn't just about proximity but about how your changing identity seeks and maintains connection.

What Loneliness Teaches You

Rather than rushing to fix or avoid loneliness, there's deep wisdom in pausing to listen to what it's trying to tell us. Loneliness isn't a flaw or a personal failing. Listening to the signal provides vital insight. Dr Bella Ingram, a psychologist specialising in life transitions, notes that loneliness often appears during key life stages — moments when your sense of self shifts and the roles that once defined you fade away. She explains that *loneliness stems from a loss of belonging, an unseen rupture between our past identity and our current self.*[4] The rupture hurts because it's real. You're not imagining the loss. But what makes it so difficult to bear is the belief that the rupture is permanent, that the gap between who you were and who you're becoming can never be bridged. In fact, loneliness is the bridge itself; it may be uncomfortable to cross, but it is essential on the journey.

This gap, though painful, opens space for new things to grow in your life. Seeing loneliness as a messenger instead of an enemy can lead you to what's missing: genuine connection, meaningful purpose, or a closer relationship with yourself. The loneliness that often comes when children leave home can signal that it's time to focus on relationships and activities outside of parenting roles. It might point you towards overlooked friendships, unexplored interests, or hidden parts of your identity.

According to research in the *Journal of Positive Psychology*, women who approached loneliness with curiosity rather than judgment were more likely to emerge from the empty nest phase with stronger social connections and a clearer sense of purpose.[5] When you accept rather than avoid the discomfort, it becomes a compass pointing toward authentic renewal.

Pathways Through Loneliness

While loneliness signals a need for your attention, it doesn't need to take hold permanently. Research-backed strategies can help you rebuild connection gradually and authentically, though it's essential to acknowledge that taking these steps can feel overwhelming when you're already struggling with isolation.

1. Rebuild Social Bonds Gradually

Connection returns through small, consistent steps rather than a major life overhaul. This advice, however, can feel frustratingly simple when you're in the depths of loneliness. Start with existing relationships: text an old friend, call a family member you've been meaning to contact, or reach out to a neighbour you've only ever waved to. When Sharon, 56, discovered her old Zumba partner on Instagram, she didn't just reminisce about their time together in the 90s. Despite neither owning a wetsuit, they signed up for a weekend stand-up paddleboard class together. Be brave. Reach out to others in whatever shape or form.

The key is consistency over intensity; regular, small interactions are more sustainable than ambitious social commitments. But don't be surprised if these first steps feel forced or artificial. Rebuilding your social connections after years of child-focused relationships takes time and patience.

2. Use Technology as a Bridge

Online communities offer valuable support, especially in remote areas or facing specific challenges. With thousands of members worldwide, Facebook's empty nest support groups connect women across different regions and generations. Elisa discovered this during her first winter alone after her twins left for university. She shared that *the 2 am conversations with women in different time zones became my anchor. Someone was always awake somewhere, understanding exactly what I meant when I said the house felt too quiet.*

However, digital connection works best when it complements rather than replaces face-to-face interaction. The goal is to use technology to facilitate genuine connection rather than substituting scrolling for socialising.

3. Reconnect with Cultural and Spiritual Communities

Returning to cultural practices or spiritual communities can give a sense of belonging and continuity. This might involve joining cultural groups, attending religious services, participating in traditional celebrations, or simply cooking ancestral meals with others from similar backgrounds. After months of eating alone, Aya started hosting monthly Lebanese cooking sessions for other mothers whose children had moved away. *The kitchen filled with Arabic once more*, she reflected. *We cooked for each other instead of sitting in empty chairs.*

These connections often provide you with the deep cultural resonance that mainstream social activities may lack, offering companionship and an understanding of the values and traditions that shape your sense of self.

4. Create Purposeful Routines

Engagement in meaningful activities helps restore social connections. This might involve taking classes, joining hobby groups, or pursuing learning opportunities you've postponed during active parenting years. After years of netball carnivals and school fundraisers, Jo, 60, signed up to volunteer at a music festival—not at the merch stand, but as an artist liaison, ferrying indie bands to the stage. *I went from discussing homework to discussing harmonics. Teenagers in bands are just as dramatic as at home, but with better stories.*

Choosing activities outside your comfort zone reignites your sense of purpose and throws you into circles you'd never otherwise meet. Think photography tours, urban foraging groups, citizen science projects, or charity treks. The key is choosing activities based on your genuine interest rather than solely for social benefits. When you engage in intrinsically rewarding activities, authentic connections often follow naturally.

5. Practice Vulnerable Honesty

The most powerful way to combat loneliness is to break the surrounding silence. Speaking openly about loneliness with a trusted friend, family member, or counsellor lessens shame and often uncovers that others have similar experiences. When Mel, 57, told her neighbour she was tired of only talking to the cat, her neighbour replied, *Want to try that new rooftop jazz bar?* Naming your loneliness opens the door, but pairing it with a specific, engaging invitation changes the atmosphere. It can be as simple as a dawn ocean swim after a sauna, a street art walk, or joining an open mic night together.

The courage to say, "I'm lonely," can be transformative for you and others carrying the same secret shame. As one woman discovered, *the moment I admitted I was struggling, three other mothers confessed they were too. We'd been suffering separately when we could have been healing together.* These practices are not quick fixes but stepping stones that help transform your loneliness from a wound into a guide.

A Bridge from Loneliness

Loneliness is a bridge. You're meant to cross it, not set up camp on it. The woman you were, primarily defined by caring for others, meets the woman you're becoming, defined increasingly by choice and desire. Both versions of you are real. The bridge connects them.

This chapter has explored loneliness not as a problem to be solved but as an experience to be acknowledged and understood. You've seen how it manifests differently across cultures and geographies, how it signals critical needs for connection and meaning, and how it can guide you toward more authentic relationships. But loneliness is only part of your story. As you learn to accept disconnection without panic and rebuild social bonds with intention rather than desperation, you create space for more profound questions.

The different pathways through loneliness naturally lead to deeper territory, questions of purpose, meaning, and self that extend beyond social connection. The next chapter explores the territory on the other side of the bridge, the profound, disorienting, ultimately liberating work of discovering who you are when no one is watching.

Reflection and Practices

Individual Reflection Prompts

- What kind of loneliness feels most familiar to you now: social, emotional, or existential? Describe how it shows up in your daily life.
- Think of one moment recently when you felt connected, even briefly. What made it meaningful?
- When loneliness whispers, "What's wrong with me?" what kinder truth could you offer yourself?

Practical Action Step – Connection Micro-Move

Choose one from this list to try in the next week:

- Send a message to someone you haven't spoken to in months.
- Extend one honest invitation (*I'm craving company— want to...?*).
- Sign up for one small group activity, online or local.
- Share aloud with a trusted friend or journal: "This week, I felt lonely when..."

Gentle Reframe Prompt

- Write this sentence and complete it: "Loneliness is telling me I need more of..."
  (Examples: laughter, purpose, deeper conversations, spiritual grounding, creative play.)

Key Takeaway

Loneliness isn't a personal flaw; it's a signal, a teacher. When we listen honestly and respond with even small steps toward connection, it becomes less an enemy to fear and more a bridge toward a new version.

Chapter 8

Renewing Identity

*S*he introduced herself at a workshop and faltered. There was no job title, no child's milestones to share, just her name. During that pause, she felt the heaviness of a question she hadn't faced in years: Who am I now? The silence felt awkward. Around her, other women rattled off their titles: CEO, mother of three, community volunteer. But she found herself searching for words that no longer suited her. "I'm... I used to be..." she started, then stopped; the identity she had held for decades no longer felt like her own.

Later, driving home through familiar countryside, she realised something profound had shifted. The woman who had once defined herself through caring for others, preparing school lunches, attending parent-teacher meetings, and coordinating family schedules was discovering that someone else had been waiting beneath all those roles. Not someone new, but someone who had been quietly growing in the spaces between all that giving. She approached this realisation with unexpected curiosity. Rather than panicking at the absence of familiar labels, she wondered: What if this emptiness wasn't loss but possibility? What if "Who am I now?" wasn't a crisis but an invitation?[1]

The invitation arrives precisely when you're least prepared to accept it, when your credentials have expired, your résumé reads like an archaeological dig, and the woman you spent decades becoming suddenly feels like a stranger wearing your clothes.

Curiosity often marks the difference between struggling indefinitely with the empty nest transition and eventually thriving.[2] Your willingness to sit with uncertainty, to explore rather than immediately fill the void, opens pathways to authentic self-discovery that rushing toward new roles cannot provide.

This unravelling doesn't happen all at once. Instead, it unfolds gradually, imperceptible at first, then undeniable. It begins in moments when you realise you've been introducing yourself through other people's accomplishments for so long that your own feel foreign. The daily structure that once provided a clear purpose slowly dissolves, leaving behind a strange new freedom that can feel both exhilarating and terrifying.[3]

You might find yourself echoing what Jasmine from Melbourne shared in a support group: *I'd been 'mum' for so long, I forgot how to be anything else.* Her words speak to the natural result of years you've shaped through love, responsibility, and the beautiful intensity of raising children. But now, as your children step confidently into their own lives, you find yourself standing at the threshold of becoming someone different.

This threshold space exists in your mind rather than the physical world. It's the uncertain territory between your familiar identity and emerging possibility. Like standing in a doorway, you can see both where you've been and glimpses of where you might go, but you belong entirely to neither space. It's neither comfortable nor permanent, but it's where the transformation takes root. Understanding why this identity shift feels so disorienting requires examining the deeper cultural currents that have shaped your sense of self over generations.

Inherited Stories

Reconstructing an identity doesn't happen in isolation. It occurs against centuries of messages about what makes a woman valuable, worthy, and good. Three generations of women might sit around your kitchen table, each carrying different scripts about identity, yet all shaped by versions of the same underlying narrative: that good women give endlessly, ask for little, and find their worth in service to others.[4]

Consider your own lineage. Perhaps your grandmother, born in the 1930s, measured success by spotless homes and well-behaved children, finding identity through domestic perfection. Your mother, coming of age in the 1960s, juggled career and family, proving women could have it all while rarely questioning whether they wanted it all. Now, at fifty-five, you stand in the kitchen your mother renovated, wondering what you want to do and who you can become.

No one tells you that the most challenging part of re-constructing identity isn't discovering who you want to be. It's permitting yourself to enjoy anything at all. Decades of selflessness don't just shape your actions. They reshape your capacity to recognise your own desires as legitimate. Each generation inherited slightly different rules, but the core message persisted: your value lies in your capacity to nurture, support, and sacrifice for others. The voice that whispers *selfish* when you consider your own desires, the guilt that accompanies any moment of rest, and your automatic assumption that everyone else's needs come first are cultural patterns passed down like family recipes.[5]

One of the most challenging aspects of shifting your identity involves confronting this deep-seated fear of selfishness. For decades, you've been praised for self-sacrifice and rewarded for putting others first. The invitation to focus on your own desires triggers alarm bells programmed over your lifetime. But claiming space for identity work isn't selfish. When you know who you are, you can offer your authentic self to relationships rather than the exhausted remnants of endless giving.

This cultural inheritance shapes how you view identity questions in our digital age, where social media creates new pressures for comparison and performance, just when your primary identity source is shifting. Combined with the sudden absence of daily mothering tasks, these inherited scripts can make the ground feel unsteady beneath your feet.

From Collapse to Curiosity

You might find it hard to confidently understand who you are right now. For many women, the empty nest resembles the aftermath of a significant disruption, when familiar landmarks have vanished and the landscape is alien. The woman who knew exactly what each day would bring and who felt indispensable begins to fade like photographs left in harsh sunlight.

Grief runs deeper than just missing your children.

You're mourning them and the version of yourself that is slipping away. You might describe this phase as psychological collapse, not a breakdown, but certainty fading. Or you might find yourself echoing what a woman from Adelaide said: *I missed the chaos, school runs, and noise. My house felt like a stranger's, and so did I.*

Yet this uncomfortable collapse makes space for something new to emerge in your life. Your identity sometimes needs to dissolve before it can bloom again. The key lies in approaching this uncertainty with curiosity rather than panic. Instead of asking "What's wrong with me?", ask "What's possible now?"

Embrace this liminal space with curiosity rather than rushing to fill the void.[6] Understand that change requires destruction and creation, release and reaching forward. When certainty dissolves, deeper parts of yourself begin to stir. But curiosity alone doesn't explain what's actually happening beneath the surface. When one identity loosens its grip, others don't simply appear.

Archetypal Awakening

Psychologist Robert Johnson's work on archetypes sheds light on what occurs during this transition. It isn't about becoming someone new; it's about allowing dormant parts of yourself to resurface: the fearless explorer who once backpacked before children arrived, the creator who loved crafting with her hands, and the mentor who naturally guided younger colleagues. These facets of you didn't vanish during intensive mothering; they waited patiently.

When Catherine's children left, she felt rudderless until therapy helped her reconnect with what Johnson might call the inner explorer. She began travelling solo to remote destinations she had only dreamed of visiting. Her journeys weren't just geographical; they were psychological expeditions that reawakened fearless, self-directed aspects of her identity that motherhood had temporarily eclipsed. You may find similar archetypal energies stirring within you.

Such archetypal shifts unfold in small, steady ways in your life. Ellen discovered her creator archetype while sorting through boxes of old baby clothes. Rather than simply donating them, she began crafting memory quilts for herself and other families navigating transitions. Through fabric and thread, she stitched together her past and her creative future, discovering that her identity wasn't just that of a mother, but also an artist. She became a woman who transforms memory into beauty. You might find your own creative expressions emerging in unexpected ways.

These archetypal energies weave your caregiving wisdom into broader expressions of self. The nurturing capacity that once focused primarily on your children might broaden to include mentoring, community service, or creative projects that serve the wider world.

Reclamation Through Small Acts

How you reconstruct your identity often begins with brief moments to yourself, the way a river finds its natural course. It starts with the smallest of choices: reading for pleasure without guilt, taking longer showers, wearing clothes that please you rather than others, and saying no without extensive justification. These seem trivial but represent profound shifts from other-focused to self-aware living.

You might start noticing your preferences: how you like your coffee, what music makes you feel alive, which colours lift your mood and what exercise brings the greatest pleasure. Family preferences and practical considerations may have overshadowed these personal tastes for years. Choosing becomes an act of self-definition, an assertion of identity.

Jane discovered this when she began mentoring young professionals re-entering the workforce. Drawing on her years of parenting experience, she developed high-level skills in problem-solving, emotional intelligence, and crisis navigation. She found she had wisdom to offer and room to grow. *I realised I hadn't lost my nurturing abilities*, she reflected. *I'd just been looking for new places to plant them.* You might find similar ways to channel your accumulated wisdom.

Wendy's transformation took a different path. When her last child left Brisbane for university, she applied for a locum position in remote Queensland. Working in a rural clinic, she discovered that being needed professionally differed from being personally required. Both were valuable, but they served different aspects of her identity. What began as filling empty days became a revelation about her capacity for adventure and professional independence. Your own path might lead in entirely different directions.

These women's stories share common threads that you might recognise in your own journey: they didn't abandon their past selves but integrated their experiences into broader identities; they allowed curiosity to guide them rather than forcing predetermined outcomes; and they recognised that identity reconstruction requires gradual work and self-compassion, not harsh judgment. Over time, small acts gather force. They don't just reclaim moments; they reshape your life, preparing the ground for wider integration.

Evolving Identity

Your goal in this transition isn't to become someone entirely different but to become someone you choose to be, a natural flowering of capabilities that were always there. This evolution requires you to integrate the wisdom you've gained through relationships with aspects of identity that were temporarily set aside.

This integration process involves mourning aspects of your identity that no longer serve you while celebrating those ready to grow. The organisational skills you've developed through managing your family might be helpful in business ventures or community leadership. Your experience in re-searching schools, activities, and resources for your children could lead to a role as a relocation consultant. The emotional intelligence you've built through parenting might guide your mentoring relationships or creative pursuits.

As you navigate this integration work, you begin speaking to yourself with the same compassion you'd offer a beloved friend. When your inner critic whispers comparisons such as *Everyone else seems to have figured this out*, you practise responding; *This is difficult work, and I'm doing my best.*

Freedom to choose your identity represents the natural evolution from external validation to internal authority. You stop seeking permission from family, society, or the imaginary audience that once dictated countless choices. You start choosing based on what feels true rather than what looks good, what energises rather than what impresses, the culmination of successfully integrating your accumulated wisdom with your authentic self. [8]

Mirrors and Horizons

Standing before the mirror, you see a face marked by time and experience. But you also recognise something hidden by years of concentrating on everyone else's reflection: eyes bright with curiosity about what comes next. The empty nest hasn't diminished you; it has revealed who you are. All the roles you played, all the care you provided, all the love you offered were expressions of who you are, not the totality of who you could become. The mother who raised confident children, the partner who built relationships, and the woman who navigated decades of responsibility remain within you. But now they're joined by the artist, the adventurer, the student, the mentor, the woman who finally has permission to take up space in her own life.

Identity in the empty nest becomes both a homecoming and a departure: returning to aspects of yourself that were temporarily set aside while embarking on aspects not yet fully explored. It's the integration of who you've been with and who you're becoming, reflected in the mirror but reaching toward the horizon.

Returning to that workshop where this chapter began, imagine yourself now, months later, at another gathering. When asked to introduce yourself, you pause, not from uncertainty, but from the pleasant difficulty of choosing which aspect of your expanding identity to share. *I'm Mel*, you might say, *and I'm still working on it.* The following silence isn't uncomfortable; it's spacious, fun and full of possibility.

A New Self

Rediscovering your identity after the children leave is about expanding rather than replacing your sense of self. The roles you once held with care and strength become part of your broader, richer story. Beneath the labels of mother, partner, daughter, or professional is a woman with her voice, preferences, dreams, and capacity for joy. The woman who emerges from this threshold isn't someone new. You are more integrated, intentional, and attuned to yourself. You haven't started over; you're continuing the conversation between who you've been and who you're becoming, with the wisdom of experience informing your new choices.

Your children may be gone, but your instincts to nurture and protect still linger. For years, they reached out, from scraped knees to school lunches and midnight fevers. Now those same instincts restlessly hover, searching for a home. The truth is, they still belong somewhere: with you.

What happens when you learn to mother yourself with the same fierceness, tenderness, and unwavering commitment you once gave to everyone else? The next chapter explores self-care as the radical, essential practice of remembering that your body matters.

Reflections and Practices

Reflection Prompts – Listening to the Self Emerging

- When you introduce yourself, which words feel outdated, and which feel alive?
- If you could whisper to the younger you who once dreamed beyond family roles, what would you remind her?

Guided Journalling Exercises
- The Mirror Dialogue: Sit with a mirror. Write a dialogue between your reflection and your inner voice. Let your reflection ask, "Who are you becoming? " Let your voice respond without censoring.

Practices for Ongoing Identity Work
Social Media Audit with Intention
- Unfollow accounts that trigger comparison.
- Follow three accounts that reflect who you're becoming (artists, writers, activists, adventurers, women in midlife).
- Experiment with posting one small thing each week that reflects you right now.

Identity Walk
On a quiet walk, repeat the question: "Who am I when no one needs me? " Notice what rises. It may be images, feelings, or memories. Record them when you return if this feels right.

Key Takeaway
Identity in the empty nest isn't about abandoning who you've been but weaving those threads into a broader, richer canvas. Every small act of curiosity, reclamation, and self-honesty helps you see that you are not beginning again. You are continuing, layered and luminous.

Chapter 9

Self-Care:
The Art of Tending to Yourself

*S*he stood in a pharmacy queue. The woman ahead bought children's vitamins and bandages, while her basket contained hormone medication she's meant to collect for weeks. In that moment, it became clear how easily she drifted from vigilant guardian of others' health to a neglectful steward of her own.

Such neglect was not carelessness but the result of years of conditioning. Caring for others became so automatic that not looking after herself almost felt virtuous. Her family was nurtured, farm paddocks tended, workers fed, and machinery serviced, yet her needs went unattended. This wasn't neglect born of laziness but of a profound cultural training: that good mothers empty themselves, that self-care is what's left over after everyone else is served. By that logic, there's never anything left over. There's never supposed to be. The same woman who reminded her daughter to eat and rest might skip meals for days without notice.

This chapter explores how to rebuild your relationship with a changing body, create environments that support your well-being, establish practices that nurture your mind and spirit, and rediscover sources of joy that may have been set aside during the busy years of parenting. It's about "mothering yourself" and involves applying the same level of attentiveness, patience, and commitment to the nurturing you undertook with your children.

The Revolutionary Nature of Self-Care

Self-care goes beyond bubble baths and scented candles. During the empty nest transition, it becomes a deep act of self-recognition, a way to affirm that you matter as a whole person, not just in relation to others. Audre Lorde's reminder that self-care is not self-indulgence but self-preservation is timely. Preservation feels essential when children leave daily life.[1]

Often, the biggest obstacle to self-care comes from within. After years of prioritising others, attending to your needs can seem selfish. These deeply rooted and conditioned beliefs might have helped you during the intensive caregiving stage, but now they require careful self-reflection. You deserve care simply because you exist, not for what you give.[2]

Relearning self-care involves consciously rewiring old habits. A useful test is the beloved child test: What care would you insist upon for a child you cherish who is tired, stressed, or unwell? That standard becomes your baseline outcome. It might mean treating a doctor's appointment with the same importance as a family commitment or protecting your morning quiet time as fiercely as your once-cherished nap times. It's about establishing sustainable systems that respect changing needs and enhance your ability to manage, without apology, for the decades to come. The practices you create now—whether routines, boundaries, or restorative habits—lay the foundation for ongoing independence, vitality, and joy as life unfolds. Once you view self-care as an essential act rather than an indulgence, the next step is to focus on the physical basis that makes everything possible: your body.

Your Physical Foundation

Physical health underpins well-being and becomes especially important during midlife, when hormonal changes affect energy, sleep, and strength. For years, your body has supported others: carrying children, staying awake through fevers, running on fumes between school runs and work deadlines. Now, you can prioritise your body's needs for the first time in years, but this requires learning to recognise long-ignored signals.

A woman on a farm only realised her chronic fatigue, disrupted sleep, and back pain after her youngest left home. The constant busyness of motherhood had hidden what her body had been trying to tell her for years. Paying attention to these signs made the patterns visible and manageable. This awakening to our body's voice marks the start of a different relationship with physical health.

For many women, the empty nest and menopause happen together, a double transition that can feel overwhelming or, unexpectedly, freeing. Actor Naomi Watts redefines menopause as a time of empowerment and renewal, challenging the cultural narrative of decline.[3] These changes go far beyond hot flushes, affecting bone density, muscle mass, mood, and energy rhythms. Embracing rather than resisting them helps maintain vitality. Monitoring your body's patterns (when energy peaks, how foods affect mood and sleep, how recovery time has increased) offers a practical way to stay informed and care for yourself.

Modern wellness tools now support this deeper listening. Wearable devices like smartwatches monitor sleep and heart health. At the same time, digital journals and online communities focused on menopause provide data and support that help women navigate midlife with greater awareness and confidence. Once we learn to attune to our changing bodies, movement becomes the most immediate way to honour that awareness.

Listening to your body is only half the conversation. The other half is responding to what you hear. For most women emerging from decades of caregiving, the body's first message is simple and urgent: move me. Not to punish or perfect, but to remember what this flesh can do when honoured rather than ignored.

Exercise

In midlife, the focus of exercise shifts fundamentally from appearance to function, from aesthetics to ability. The goal becomes maintaining the strength to carry groceries, climb stairs, and easily rise from the floor. These practical capabilities safeguard independence and quality of life in the years ahead.

Strength training becomes critical after forty-five to protect bone density, preserve muscle, and support balance. Bodyweight exercises, resistance bands, yoga, and Pilates all build strength in accessible and sustainable ways. Even everyday activities contribute: gardening provides natural lifting and squatting, while household tasks build functional fitness. Walking remains one of the most effective cardiovascular and mental health activities, especially when paired with resistance or weight-bearing exercise.

Modern science highlights the importance of mobility and balance training. Simple practices like single-leg stands while brushing teeth or light stretching before bed reduce fall risk and maintain movement confidence. Apps, online classes, and community programs tailored for women in midlife make it easier than ever to learn safe, effective routines from home.

Movement nourishes much more than just muscle and bone. A morning walk in nature, across fields, parks, or lakes, can serve as meditation, connecting body and earth while providing space for reflection. Those early morning walks that once seemed impossible to fit in? They're now yours. Dance classes, swimming, and cycling groups blend social connection with physical vitality. Consistency matters more than intensity. The aim is sustained movement that feels doable and enjoyable.

Nutrition

Alongside movement and sleep, nutrition forms the third pillar of midlife wellbeing. Hormonal changes during perimenopause and menopause alter how the body uses energy, stores fat, and maintains muscle, transforming food choices into long-term investments in strength and vitality.

When you're no longer cooking for growing teenagers or accommodating picky eaters, your relationship with food can finally shift. You can cook for one, experiment with foods that nourish you specifically, and eat at times that suit your body's rhythms rather than the school timetable.

Protein helps preserve muscle, while calcium and vitamin D are vital for bone health. Fibre, whole grains, and healthy fats benefit heart health. Simple changes like adding legumes, nuts, and leafy greens can have lasting effects. Emerging research highlights the gut-brain connection: a balanced microbiome aids digestion, mood, immunity, and sleep.[4] Fermented foods, diverse plant fibres, and enough hydration support gut health in powerful ways.

Nutrition experts like Dr Joanna McMillan[5] and the Jean Hailes Foundation for Women's Health[6] emphasise that nutrition in midlife is about enjoyment, nourishment, and building resilience for the decades ahead. Yet even with optimal nutrition and regular movement, the body cannot thrive without adequate rest.

Sleep

Quality sleep becomes more crucial and complex during hormonal changes. Poor rest disrupts the hormones that regulate energy, mood, and immunity, setting off a chain reaction that hampers every other aspect of health. Consistent sleep routines—such as cool, dark bedrooms, relaxing wind-down rituals, and device-free evenings—help support the deeper rest our changing bodies require.

The house is quieter now. No midnight teenager returns, no early morning alarms for school runs. This silence, once painful, becomes a gift: the chance to establish sleep patterns that serve you rather than accommodate everyone else's schedules.

Many women discover their best sleep after removing phones from the bedroom, which frees the mind from late-night scrolling and social media anxiety. Simple boundaries with technology help the nervous system prepare for rest and restore natural circadian rhythms.

The body regains remarkable strength when movement, nourishment, and rest harmonise. Attending to these physical foundations provides the energy and stability needed for the emotional healing and creative journeys ahead. This is not self-indulgence; it's reclamation. Your body carried you through the intense years of motherhood. Now it deserves your attention, care, and gratitude. With physical needs thoughtfully met, space naturally opens for rediscovering identity, purpose, and joy.

Tending Your Inner Landscape

For years, your focus has been outward; caring, organising, anticipating the needs of others. Now the invitation is to turn that same attentiveness inward. Glennon Doyle suggests that our job throughout life is to disappoint as many people as possible to avoid disappointing ourselves.[7] That may sound bold, but it is also liberating. For years, disappointing yourself wasn't just acceptable: it was expected, even praised. The 'good mother' badge came with a hidden cost: your own needs ranked last, always. Now the revolutionary work is unlearning the belief that you're selfish for having needs.

Self-care is an act of recognition, a declaration that your inner world matters. A good first step is matching your care to your natural energy rather than old family timetables. One of the greatest gifts of the empty nest years is the freedom to work with your energy rather than constantly bending to family schedules. You may thrive as an early riser, or your creativity blooms late at night. Some women discover they need an afternoon pause, not as a luxury but as a natural rhythm. Honouring these patterns brings not only more productivity but also more satisfaction. Here is a simple real-world glimpse of what that can look like.

A Perth nurse, for example, realised her sharpest, most creative hours were between 5 and 7 am. For years, she had spent those quiet moments scrolling through her phone. When she started writing during that time, she described it as reclaiming the best part of her day. She hadn't magically become a "morning person." She had chosen to protect her natural energy for what mattered most. You can find your version by paying attention to your rhythms over time.

Try tracking your energy for a week: notice when you feel most alert, when your concentration dips, and how different activities impact your vitality. Use this insight to plan your day; schedule challenging tasks or essential conversations when you're at your best and allow yourself to rest when your body asks for it. Rest becomes transformative: an early night, a midday nap, or even a quiet day of reflection can reset your nervous system and spark new creativity. Small practices can be woven gently with your day, shaped to fit you.

Small Moments, Deep Impact

Self-care doesn't need to involve big blocks of time or expensive retreats. It can be woven gently into everyday life. Morning coffee becomes a moment of gratitude. Skincare is a gentle blessing. A drive to work turns into breathing space.

Moments grow stronger when they attach to routines you already keep.

These practices become even more powerful when paired with *habit stacking*, which involves anchoring new rituals onto existing routines.[8] Deep breathing while the kettle boils, repeating affirmations while washing dishes, or recording a quick voice memo in the car can shift an ordinary moment into an act of renewal. One woman described her five-minute voice notes *as therapy with me*, which helped her move through difficult days with perspective and compassion. The goal is not to add more tasks but to bring intention into the ones you already do. Being more mindful about what you do and being present, even in the simplest routines, can become grounding, restorative acts. Alongside new habits, how you speak to yourself shapes your feelings.

The way you speak to yourself matters. Too often, the inner voice is critical: *You're falling apart.* What if, instead, it became a companion? *This feels hard. What do you need right now?* Positivity is about extending the same kindness to yourself that you would to a dear friend. When kindness to yourself needs extra support, professional help may be required.

Therapy is no longer just a last resort. It is increasingly regarded as part of regular mental health upkeep. In Australia, Medicare offers up to ten subsidised mental health sessions each year, and telehealth now makes counselling accessible even for women in rural areas. A skilled therapist can help you untangle complex emotions and provide strategies for moving forward. Asking for help is wise. Care also involves protecting your health through connection, not only through solo practices.

Research shows that loneliness in midlife carries real health risks, almost as damaging as smoking.[9] As we explored in Chapter 7, connection with others is not optional but essential. But here, quality matters far more than quantity. Choose relationships that nourish you rather than those that drain your energy. Putting that into practice often means rethinking where your time and attention go.

This may involve declining invitations that feel like obligations and spending time with people who lift you up. It might mean joining groups related to your emerging interests rather than sticking to circles centred around your children. Moving towards a self-directed social life makes space for more genuine, sustaining bonds. Honesty strengthens those connections. Sharing openly about your grief, questions of identity, or excitement for new possibilities fosters intimacy and reminds others they are not alone in their transitions. Vulnerability is not weakness; it is the foundation where stronger, more supportive relationships develop. Chapters 12 and 13 will explore this theme further.

Rediscovering Joy

Self-care paves the way to joy, though many women feel like strangers to their own sources of happiness. The path back to personal fulfilment is deeply personal, but some common themes emerge: creativity, nature, meaningful contribution, and genuine self-expression consistently nourish the soul.

Rediscovering joy starts with creativity, not as a luxury or indulgence, but as a core way of expressing oneself. Creativity is within every woman, waiting to be expressed through writing, movement, colour, sound, or meaningful conversation. Often, the journey begins with simple curiosity, like dusting off an old instrument, joining a class, or trying recipes that match changing tastes. The emphasis shifts from mastery to expression, from perfection to exploration.

Think of the teacher who discovered pottery at her local community centre after long days of marking papers. The moment clay first yielded beneath her hands, she felt a relief she hadn't realised she desperately needed. Thursday evenings became sacred: two hours where she was neither wife, mother, nor professional, but simply a woman creating something beautiful. What started as a distraction grew into meditation, with each bowl and mug becoming a quiet statement of self-worth.

Similarly, another woman, suddenly free from decades of catering to her family's food preferences, began cooking solely for herself for the first time in twenty years. Her kitchen became a lab of flavours and experiments, where forgotten spices were brought back to life and culinary mistakes turned into discoveries. Cooking shifted from merely an obligation to nourish both body and soul.

Creative expression becomes a ritual of agency, reconnecting women with curiosity, play, and the deep satisfaction of creating something with their hands. Here, process matters far more than the final product, providing stress relief, mindful presence, and reconnecting with long-neglected aspects of the self.

While creativity offers one path to happiness, perhaps even more meaningful is rediscovering pleasure in life's simplest moments. Joy often shows up in everyday experiences:

the calm quiet of early morning, choosing dinner without argument, or reading a book from start to finish without interruption. These simple freedoms can feel truly revolutionary after years of constant planning and negotiation.

One woman found unexpected joy in solo grocery shopping, finally free to go at her own pace, read food labels carefully, and choose items based solely on her preferences. Seemingly ordinary choices became powerful symbols of independence and self-determination.

Morning walks can become healing rituals. With more time to notice, women describe seeing familiar trees in a new light, hearing individual bird calls instead of background noise, and watching seasons change across landscapes they had walked past but never truly observed. What initially felt like loneliness often became a deep connection between nature and themselves.

Whether through creative expression or simple daily pleasures, the secret is not in dismissing these experiences as insignificant but in celebrating and cultivating them intentionally. A life built around such joyful moments creates sustainable happiness, rooted less in external validation and more in gratitude, awareness, and presence. Rediscovering joy marks the beginning of a life lived more fully for oneself, grounded in authentic pleasure and genuine self-care.

Cultural Practices as Healing

Self-care also stems from cultural traditions, connecting personal wellness to heritage, identity, and community. Australia's multicultural society offers many avenues: tai chi in parks, Indigenous bushwalks that teach about plants, community yoga, or craft circles that celebrate traditional skills while building friendships. One woman joined a community garden inspired by her Italian roots. Growing food and sharing harvests with neighbours combined movement, connection, and cultural pride. Her grandmother's words about dirt under the fingernails being a sign of a life well-lived took on new meaning as ancestral wisdom guided her modern practice.

For others, healing involves learning about native plants from Indigenous educators, taking part in cultural cooking classes, or joining music circles that nurture creativity and a sense of belonging. These activities feel like coming home, blending self-care with identity, tradition, and shared meaning. Cultural practices also provide rhythm and structure, reminding us that self-care benefits more than just ourselves. Caring for your vitality strengthens your family, friendships, and community.

Personal Care Systems

Sustainable self-care means creating systems that fit your personality, lifestyle, and circumstances, rather than copying someone else's approach. If you prefer routine, focus on consistent practices that bring stability. If you thrive on variety, build around principles and values that can take different forms depending on your needs and interests.

Consider creating a personal care protocol —a set of practices that support your well-being throughout various stages of life. This isn't about rigid checklists but rhythms, small anchors across your days, weeks, and months that remind you that you matter. Daily anchors might include taking medications, moving your body, and eating nourishing food. Weekly routines could involve social connection, preparing for the week, or activities that bring joy. Monthly practices might include checking your physical and emotional health, seeing what's working, and setting new intentions.

Choose practices that match your core values, not fleeting ideals. This might mean enjoying morning walks rather than gym sessions, chatting with a close mate instead of attending big social gatherings, or gardening instead of taking meditation classes.

Adjusting to the seasons is wisdom. Needs shift with energy levels, health, and even the weather. Summer may call for early outdoor walks and light meals, while winter may invite slower mornings, warm baths, and nourishing soups. Flexibility is a strength as it shows self-awareness and responsiveness.

Set aside time to check how your self-care is going. Ask yourself: Do I have steady energy most days? Do I feel connected to those who matter? Can I handle everyday stress without feeling overwhelmed? These reflections help you make adjustments before small issues become bigger problems. Sometimes, you might need more rest, and other times, more activity or connection. Sometimes for solitude, other times for community. The goal is to develop self-care that suits your current situation.

Regular reviews also allow you to celebrate progress. Acknowledging improvements in your health, relationships, or satisfaction builds confidence and shows which practices benefit you. This helps you focus your energy where it matters most.

Laying the Foundation

The empty nest years invite a shift from giving everything outward to finally turning that same devotion inward. Self-care is no longer an afterthought or occasional indulgence but a foundation for strength, vitality, and joy. By listening to your body, tending your mind, and honouring your needs, you build resilience for decades ahead.

This chapter has shown that self-care can be practical through movement, sleep, nutrition, energy awareness, and soulful through creativity, daily joy, and cultural connection. What matters most is responsiveness, perfection, and authenticity rather than imitation. The practices you choose today become small, steady investments in your future self, shaping how you live, age, and thrive.

In the next chapter, we explore what happens when caring for yourself creates room for freedom: the small daily decisions that gradually reshape everything, the reclamation of time as yours, and the radical discovery that you can finally live for yourself without apology.

Reflections and Practices

Individual Reflection Prompts
Emotional Processing

- Think of a recent small act of care you gave yourself: a care visit, a walk, a rest. How did it shift your mood?
- What emotions arise when you hear I matter too?

Creative Journalling Exercises
Mapping Your Care

- Draw a wheel divided into six segments: Body, Mind,

Emotions, Creativity, Rest, Connection. In each, write one way you currently tend to yourself and one way you'd like to expand.

Ongoing Check-Ins

- This week, what's one nourishing act I did for my body?
- What small joy surprised me today?
- Did I protect any time just for myself? How did it feel?

Partner/Group Discussion Prompts

- Which self-care practices can we share (walks, meals, rituals) and which are best protected as solo?

Key Takeaway

Self-care in the empty nest years is not a luxury but a birthright, an everyday practice of tending to yourself with the same love you once gave everyone else.

Chapter 10

Freedom: The Psychological Gifts

After years of school schedules, family routines, and the relentless choreography of managing other lives, a strange lightness crept in. She slept in. There was no alarm, no children rushing through, no work, no apologies. She lay still, unsure whether it felt luxurious or lonely. She had nothing urgent to get up for, so she stayed in bed for the morning, listening to the walls groan as they adjusted to the heat. She could choose her day without consultation, compromise, or negotiation for the first time in years. Being unfamiliar with this idea, it took her all day to decide what she wanted. So, she chose to do nothing.

The same lightness appeared on her daily walks along farm tracks with an audiobook or podcast and on country bike rides. There was no one to answer to, no one to check in with, no timeline but her own. Freedom emerged from all directions, showing up on a Tuesday with an SBS film and again on a Saturday while reading a book on the couch.

What starts as a lightness in daily routines quickly shows up in the smallest choices, turning even a shopping trip into an unexpected moment of confronting freedom. This chapter examines how such a mental shift happens in the tiniest daily moments. It's not about the freedom of imagination but the habit of living with decisions made each day, deliberately and for yourself alone.

Albert Camus wrote, *Freedom is nothing but a chance to be better.*[1] That 'better' isn't about achievement or productivity in the empty nest. It's about becoming more yourself, more aligned with your authentic preferences, more attuned to your natural rhythms, more honest about what brings you genuine satisfaction.

Gift of Choice

Freedom slips in quietly through everyday moments that may feel odd and meaningful. For decades, your preferences were background noise to everyone else's needs. Now they're the only voice in the room, and you've almost forgotten how to hear them. Freedom comes with silence, asking you to fill it with something that matters to you alone.

Life adjusts in countless small ways. Dinner can happen anytime, be any meal, or be skipped without explanation. You could spend Saturday morning in bed with coffee and newspapers, in the garden, or driving to the coast without checking schedules or coordinating logistics. You can pull out that old sewing machine and see if it still works.

This sudden sense of freedom is exhilarating for some and overwhelming for others, especially women who are used to constant negotiation. Decision fatigue arises not from too many obligations but from too many choices. Simple questions may feel challenging: What do I want? What brings me joy?

The learning curve is steep but profoundly transformative. Each decision made solely for personal satisfaction, like taking the scenic route home, buying expensive tea, or reading fiction into the dead of night, becomes a small act of self-recognition. These choices, accumulated over weeks and months, rebuild something vital: trust in your personal judgment and the right to prioritise your individual needs.

Freedom is shaped just as much by what is no longer there as by what remains. The peaceful house, the untouched fridge, and the folded towels all serve as reminders of what has been let go.

What's Gone

Freedom often begins with noticing what isn't there anymore. The stillness upon waking becomes remarkable. The kitchen remains tidy overnight, with no late-night raids or dishes appearing mysteriously in the sink. The fridge contains the same items as yesterday. Your shampoo stays precisely where you left it, an almost miraculous consistency after decades of family life.

These might seem trivial, but they reveal something profound: reclaiming physical and mental space. As clutter clears, so does the mental noise from constantly managing others' needs, emotions, and schedules. The fridge hums quietly, untouched by slamming doors. Towels stay neatly folded. Hot water lasts for your entire shower.

Days now pass smoothly as natural rhythms replace imposed schedules.[2] Spontaneity returns: a twilight jog along a peaceful trail decided on impulse, a last-minute weekend escape booked without checking multiple calendars, an afternoon fully dedicated to whatever moves you.

The Return of Mental Territory

There comes a moment when your thoughts no longer compete with mental to-do lists and teenage emotional weather. The constant background hum of family management gradually fades, leaving space for different thinking to emerge.

You might head out to feed the chickens, completely forget what you went for, and then feel amused when you realise you've been lost in thoughts about stars. Once seen as a distraction, this kind of mental wandering proves to be a gift, the return of imagination to its natural state.[3] An entire afternoon might disappear into pondering questions with no practical application: What would cities look like if designed by artists? How do other cultures understand time? Why do certain colour combinations feel emotionally satisfying? These mental excursions, forbidden luxuries during intensive parenting years, become daily possibilities.

Books reappear on your bedside table, not parenting guides or educational resources, but novels chosen purely for pleasure. You finish reading them. A journal emerges from a forgotten drawer. Ideas long set aside drift back, patient and persistent, asking to be explored. It could be a podcast that challenges long-held assumptions, or quiet moments spent reflecting on art, politics, or philosophy. The quality of your attention changes, too. Where once everything felt urgent, hurried and surface-level, now there is time for deeper consideration. Problems can be turned over slowly, examined from multiple angles, discussed with trusted friends, or left to marinate until clarity emerges naturally.

Once colonised by family life, this psychological territory

becomes available for personal exploration. The mental space to wonder, question, imagine, and dream proves as precious as any physical room in the house. This restoration of imagination gradually reshapes how time itself is experienced.

Living by Internal Rhythms

Learning to trust natural rhythms takes practice. Some days call for focused activity and accomplishment, while others demand rest, reflection, or gentle pleasure. Your energy levels fluctuate with seasons, hormones, and life circumstances. When you learn to work with these patterns rather than against them, you often discover greater satisfaction and sustained vitality.

Sarah, a Sydney mother, joined a local book club after her sons left home. She discovered she could arrive early for deeper conversations with other members, linger afterwards to discuss personal reflections, and read at whatever pace felt natural without stealing time from other responsibilities. *I had not read for pleasure in years, she reflected. Now I remember what it feels like to lose myself entirely in a story, to think about characters and ideas long after closing the book.* The rhythm became hers to design, shaped by interest rather than obligation.

The Authority of Inner Voice

With your household's emotional volume turned down, something long buried emerges: your inner voice's quiet yet persistent authority. You may have operated on autopilot for years, responding to family crises, celebrations, and daily needs before your own thoughts fully formed. The empty nest creates space for internal conversation to resume. When it first emerges, this inner dialogue can feel rusty and unsure. What matters to me now? What brings genuine satisfaction instead of just completing tasks?

The process often begins with small preferences asserting themselves. You develop strong opinions about art, politics, and travel destinations. Working from home, you might suddenly notice how light falls across your living room at different times of day. Interests that lay dormant begin stirring again, asking for attention and exploration.[4] Small exercises in self-determination rebuild something crucial: confidence in your judgment, knowing what feels right, what nourishes, and what depletes your energy, and the courage to honour those insights without lengthy explanations or apologies.

A former teacher, Julie, describes it as remembering that she has complex thoughts about the world beyond her immediate family's needs. She stayed up late reading about subjects that had interested her, yet she had never had time to pursue, like astronomy, poetry, and sustainable agriculture. She reflects that she had forgotten she was curious about ideas that served no practical purpose in family life but fed something essential in her.

Small Rebellions

This new freedom is a subtle rebellion against years of budgeting, compromise, and accommodation. These are acts of personal preference that accumulate into something meaningful. You might buy the expensive olive oil you've always wanted but couldn't justify when feeding a family. You rearrange furniture to catch better morning light, even though the old setup was more practical for family gatherings. You choose the restaurant you prefer rather than the one your children usually pick, and relax over your meal without checking the time or managing anyone else's needs.

The rebellion extends to social expectations, too. You begin declining invitations that feel like duty rather than pleasure, choosing instead to protect time for activities that genuinely interest you. You stop pretending to enjoy particular social gatherings and start seeking out people who share your emerging interests rather than your parenting history. Sometimes rebellion involves reclaiming neglected parts of yourself. The music you enjoyed before having children returns to daily life. The clothing style you preferred before practical family considerations dominated wardrobe choices makes a comeback. The political opinions you softened to maintain family harmony can be expressed more freely again.

These acts of gentle defiance, accumulated over time, create something powerful: a life that reflects authentic preferences rather than accumulated compromises. They mark your transition from living primarily for others to living primarily from personal truth.[5]

Freedom as Foundation

This psychological freedom creates a foundation for whatever comes next. Liz, whose children left two years ago, describes it as *finally having permission to waste time productively*. She spends her Sunday mornings reading philosophy, not because it's useful, but because it fascinates her. She takes long walks without a destination. She sits in cafes, people-watching. None of this 'accomplishes' anything, yet all of it nourishes something essential. This is the gift of freedom: the space to be curious without requiring immediate practical application.

When you reclaim time, space, and autonomy, the ripple effects extend beyond the individual. Families often benefit from more fulfilled and self-directed mothers. Communities gain from women who contribute from choice rather than obligation. Society enriches when half its population is freed to pursue new interests and express talents. This inner revolution becomes the cornerstone for all the freedoms that follow. With psychological space reclaimed, other territories open naturally: the freedom to reimagine relationships without the buffer of children's immediate needs, to move through the world guided by personal desire rather than family logistics, and to pursue work that fulfils rather than merely sustains.

The empty nest reveals that you are a whole person with interests, opinions, dreams, and desires that exist independently of your caregiving role. This realisation doesn't diminish your love for your children or your pride in the parenting journey. Instead, it adds dimension and depth, making the space for fully expressing your personality and potential.

Permission to Begin

The goal isn't about becoming selfish but about recognising your needs and desires in daily decisions regarding time and energy. Some women embrace this permission immediately, diving into postponed dreams with enthusiasm and relief. Others approach it cautiously, testing the waters of self-focus before committing to bigger changes. Both approaches are valid. The transformation timing is your own, influenced by personality, circumstances, and readiness for change. What matters most is recognising that this permission exists.. The freedom to explore who you might become beyond motherhood is a developmental necessity rather than a selfish indulgence. The space to choose your adventure is the main event rather than a consolation prize.

Earned Freedom

This hard-won psychological freedom of the empty nest, earned through years of dedication to others, creates space for the full expression of personality, interests, and potential that may have been constrained during intensive parenting years. As this internal liberation takes root, it naturally seeks expression in the world around you. Physical spaces begin to shift and evolve, relationships deepen and change, and new adventures become possible.

However, it all begins here, in the revolutionary act of thinking, feeling your emotions, and choosing your own rhythm. The following chapters examine how this inner freedom extends outward, transforming home, relationships, work, and purpose. Yet, the foundation remains steady: your right to live genuinely, to choose knowingly, and to embrace the full complexity of yourself beyond caregiving roles.

Freedom in the empty nest is both a practical gift and a philosophical invitation. It's a chance to discover what becomes possible when you finally live for yourself.

But freedom needs a container. It needs walls that reflect rather than restrict, spaces that support rather than suffocate. The psychological freedom you've reclaimed now calls for physical expression: rooms that mirror your evolving self, surfaces that hold your emerging dreams, light that falls where you place it. The next chapter explores how your home becomes the physical expression of the freedom you've earned: not a museum of the past, but a sanctuary for who you're becoming.

Reflections and Practices

Creative Journalling Exercises

- Freedom Map: Draw a map of your week as it used to be when your children were home, and another of your current week. What space has opened? What could that space hold?
- Permission Slip: Write a page that begins with *I permit myself to…* and keep going until you surprise yourself.
- Creative Archaeology: Journal about one creative impulse from your past (art, writing, music, gardening, etc.). What stopped you then? What could it look like to revisit it now?

Embodied Practices

- Time Texture: Set aside one day to let your natural energy guide you rather than the clock. Note when you rise, when you rest, when you feel curious.
- Small Experiments: Rearrange one corner of your home to reflect who you are now—a reading chair, a sketchbook on the table, or a vase of fresh flowers placed just for you.
- Freedom Walk: Take a walk without a destination or time limit. Let your mind drift. Notice where your thoughts go when they are not tethered.

Key Takeaway

True freedom in the empty nest is not just the absence of obligation, but the presence of spaciousness, curiosity, and self-determination, the chance to live on your own terms and rediscover who you are becoming.

Chapter 11

Creating a Sanctuary

She stood in the spare room, staring at the sports bags still perched on the top shelf: hockey sticks, fluorescent balls, shin guards, and the faint but persistent whiff of old socks. Stacked around them were old school files, abandoned laptops, and bags of outgrown clothes, layered over even older bundles from daycare: baby rugs, cot sheets, precious artworks, and tiny dresses she could never bring herself to part with.

She wasn't ready to let go of those snippets of memories, but something deep inside told her that the house and she needed to breathe again. The house had been everyone's home for so long that it had forgotten how to be hers. Now, with antique white paint spreading across the walls, she was teaching it a new language: beauty, deliberate comfort, space designed for one person's pleasure rather than five people's compromise.

She began unearthing decades of family life. She emptied drawers with reverent care, sorted through wardrobes like she was curating a museum, and filled packing crates with school-books and letters to return to her daughters when ready. She folded away baby clothes with infinite tenderness, saving them for when new little lives might arrive.

Each change felt like a step forward. She replaced heavy

curtains with Roman blinds, laid fresh floors that felt cool under bare feet, and finally updated the kitchen that had served two generations but never quite suited her aesthetic. Morning light streamed through the lounge room, bouncing off pale walls with a golden glow that felt unmistakably like a beginning. She installed exterior party lights so it always seemed to people travelling down that country road that life existed in that lonely house.

Fresh flowers appeared on surfaces, picked from the wild or bought as a treat. The garden, once so carefully tended by her mother-in-law, fell to neglect while raising young children and only now flourishes again under patient care and attention. Candles flickered in the evenings. White linen cushions stayed miraculously clean.

The children's bedrooms remained deliberately untouched, waiting for their return. She wasn't trying to erase their presence but create a home that felt genuinely alive again, a place that reflected the person she was becoming. That was the hard part. When they all came home simultaneously, they all wanted their original bedrooms.

Your Space, Your Terms

Whether you live in a rented apartment, a coastal cottage, or even temporary accommodation, your space matters because it's where you live. Reinvention isn't about ownership, large budgets, or expansive square footage. You are creating your own safe and secure place, where you want to come home, with an atmosphere that feels authentically yours.

Janet realised this after moving into a small rental following her divorce. She recalls having almost nothing, but she found a beautiful wingback chair at a garage sale for thirty dollars. She placed it by the window, added a soft throw from an op shop, and created her daily space away from the world. *Every morning with my coffee there, I felt like I was choosing myself.*

Some changes require investment, such as new flooring, fresh paint, or updated appliances. However, transformation often occurs through subtle moves that fit within any budget. A grandmother refreshed her retirement village unit with fairy lights strung across her small balcony and three terracotta pots of herbs. *It felt like having my own secret garden,* she says. The total cost was just a bit more than a good bottle of wine, but the emotional return was priceless.

Home decorating expert Melissa Michaels, who recently navigated her empty nest transition by downsizing to a coastal cottage, perfectly captured this approach in her book *Love the Home You Have*. She argues that creating a sanctuary isn't about designer perfection but about homes that feel lived in and deeply personal.[1] This mindset offers freedom for empty nesters reimagining their space: your home doesn't need to impress anyone anymore. It just needs to feel like yours.

Designing with Intention

Before reaching for paintbrushes, pause and reflect. What do you want this space to feel like? Do you have a theme in mind? Perhaps calm and grounding, like a coastal dawn. Vibrant and creative, bursting with colour. Or cozy and intimate, perfect for quiet evenings.

Walk through each room with fresh eyes, asking yourself how you want to feel there. Your answers become a kind of compass, guiding every choice, from colour palettes to lighting. Choose textiles that invite touch, fabrics that welcome you to sink in at the end of a long day. Notice how different colours shift your mood and trust those instincts over the glossy pages of design magazines.

Your home should engage all the senses. Natural elements often anchor this beautifully. Warm timber, organic shapes, and layered textures create an atmosphere of calm. Bridgette, for example, filled a woven basket with shells she collected during her weekly beach walks. Their soft curves caught the morning light and linked her dining room to moments of peace and solitude. Consider sound as well. Does your home feel hushed and serene, or lively with gentle activity? Soft fabrics absorb harsh echoes, while timber floors and stone surfaces amplify music or conversation. Every detail shapes the emotional tone of your rooms. The next step is straightforward once you know how you want your home to feel. Let go of what no longer supports that vision.

The Art of Gentle Release

Start with emotionally neutral items, such as old appliances, duplicate kitchen tools, or clothes that no longer match your style. These choices build momentum and confidence for tackling tougher decisions later. Remember, decluttering isn't about creating a minimalist, perfect space. It's about making room for the life you want now. Keep what brings you joy, serves a genuine purpose, or connects you to treasured memories. Let go of things that feel heavy with obligation or no longer reflect who you're becoming. Marie Kondo's well-known idea of keeping only what "sparks joy" has helped many see this process differently.[2]

Children's possessions require extra tenderness. Treasured items can be packed into carefully labelled boxes and transformed into gifts to return when children establish their own homes. This approach shifts the experience from accepting what is to giving forward, maintaining connection while creating necessary breathing space.

When one mother finally addressed her daughter's room two years after departure, she was paralysed in the doorway. Every item carried memory: netball trophies, boy band posters that had become ironically vintage, a desk covered in stickers from long-ago holidays. The prospect of change felt like erasure, like announcing that her daughter no longer lived there and the family was moving on without her.

A friend's question sparked a breakthrough: was the childhood in that room or in her heart? The question reshaped everything. She carefully packed her daughter's treasures into labelled boxes for future use, donated toys to local families, where they might bring joy to other children. She painted the room a soft grey; her daughter once mentioned wanting her future space. The realisation dawned that she wasn't erasing childhood but thoughtfully preserving it while both of them grew. When her daughter visited months later, she adored the transformation, noting it felt like home but not like she was still twelve.

Some items are hard to categorise: baby clothes that feel impossible to let go of, artwork that no longer fits current taste but holds deep emotional significance. A "maybe" pile can assist with these items. Storing them temporarily and revisiting after six months often provides the clarity needed to decide what should stay.

This gentle archaeology of your family life mirrors your internal process of releasing outdated roles while preserving what remains meaningful. Each decision becomes practice in trusting your judgment about what serves your life now, helping you feel lighter emotionally as your physical space opens. Creativity can flow in with space opening, even on the smallest budget.

Creative Transformation on Any Budget

The empty nest offers something special: the freedom to reimagine how spaces are used. Areas once dedicated to homework or toy storage can change to meet your current needs. A child's playroom might become a yoga studio, writing nook, or guest room. Jenny turned her son's old space into a craft corner on a tight budget. She kept his desk, painted it bright white, and placed fabric scraps and paintbrushes where homework used to be. *It cost me twenty dollars for paint and felt like reclaiming a part of myself I'd forgotten.*

Designers like Leanne Ford often remind us that these transformations don't need polish but gain beauty from reflecting the evolving lives of the people within them.[3] Even tiny changes can shift a room's entire energy. Position a comfortable sofa to catch the afternoon's sea breeze, instantly creating a fresh reading sanctuary. Replace harsh overhead lighting with warm table lamps, creating intimate pools of light throughout your space.

Community resources often uncover unexpected treasures. Jane searched online marketplace groups and neighbourhood swap events, eventually discovering a vintage sofa lounge she reupholstered in vibrant emerald fabric. *It became my throne,* she laughs, *where I feel most like myself.* Mason jars become stylish candle holders. Wooden crates turn into rustic shelves. Old scarves can be repurposed as table runners or wall hangings. These projects help stretch budgets while making spaces feel personal (each piece tells a story of resourcefulness and purpose). Over time, these small sanctuaries build into a larger transformation, shifting your rooms and sense of self.

Living Reflections

Reinventing your home, like reconstructing an identity, goes beyond aesthetic choices. It's a statement of who you're becoming, a declaration of what matters to you now, and a decision made for yourself rather than for others.

Six months after painting that spare room, she hosted her daughters for Christmas. They noticed immediately. *Mum, it looks fantastic,* her youngest said. *It feels like... you.* She hadn't realised how much she'd been waiting for their approval. Their recognition that the house, like her, was evolving but still theirs, still home, released something she'd been holding.

The next chapter explores how reclaiming your spaces opens up new possibilities for connection that you couldn't have imagined when the nest was full: partnerships that grow stronger when children are no longer the buffer, friendships that thrive when you finally have space to be truly present, and a new relationship with your adult children based on mutual respect rather than daily dependence.

Reflections and Practices
Personal Reflection Prompts
1. Walk through your home and notice which rooms belong to an earlier chapter. What emotions do these spaces hold?
2. Ask yourself: How do I want to feel in each main room? Energised, calm, creative, or connected?
3. Reflect on one object that feels impossible to part with. What memory does it carry? How might you honour it while still making space for your present life?

Creative Journalling Exercises
- Memory Archaeology: Choose one drawer or box to sort through. Journal the memories it evokes, and decide whether to keep, release, or gift items forward.
- Design Compass: Sketch or list words that describe the atmosphere you long for in your home (e.g., light, warmth, colour, texture). Use this as your guide when making changes.

Practical Experiments
- Create a micro-sanctuary—a chair, windowsill, or corner that feels yours. Add one element (a cushion, plant, or lamp) that shifts the mood immediately.
- Try a gentle release practice: put one sentimental item in a "maybe" box. Revisit it after six months and notice how your feelings have changed.

Key Takeaway

Creating a sanctuary is not about design trends or perfection but about shaping a home honouring your past while reflecting who you are becoming.

Chapter 12

Relationships: Partners

The dining room glowed under the pendant light, its warmth spreading over the polished jarrah table. Across from her sat her partner of forty years, and for the first time in what felt like decades, she could truly see him, not as a co-parent but as the man she'd chosen all those years ago, now emerging from behind the curtain of family life as if coming back into focus.

The clink of forks against plates punctuated a silence that felt both heavy and unfamiliar. The absence of children's voices created a space that pressed against their skin like a cool evening breeze. She studied his face with quiet wonder. When had those laugh lines deepened? How had she missed the silver threading through his hair, the way his hands moved with such familiar grace? The years of raising children blurred him into the background and reduced him to logistics and shared tasks. Somewhere in the exhausting choreography of parenthood, she'd stopped seeing the person and saw only the role.

Now, the empty nest had revealed the intricate threads of their shared life: some strong, some frayed, all demanding the attention she hadn't known how to give. But at that moment, she felt something she'd almost forgotten. Who was he now? Who had he been all along, beneath his fatherhood role? And *more unsettling still: who was she to him?*

When your children leave home, relationships don't continue as they have been. The empty nest becomes a revealing mirror, magnifying dynamics that busy family life once obscured. For some couples, this quiet creates space for rediscovery. For others, it exposes emotional distances that years of shared logistics had masked.

Discovering Each Other Again

Many couples enter the empty nest phase feeling like strangers sharing a house. The scaffolding that once held their days together vanishes almost overnight, and what remains can feel startlingly unfamiliar.

Mike and Laura, together for 28 years, felt this disorientation keenly. *Once our daughters left,* Laura reflected, *our conversations became awkward. We'd literally run out of things to say by dessert.* The couple started taking evening walks through their suburban neighbourhood, letting the eucalyptus-scented air and rhythm of walking in step gradually rebuild their connection. Mike added, *We had to learn to be curious about each other again.* These small rituals (sharing observations about a neighbour's garden, discovering new music) became the foundation for rediscovering intimacy beyond parenting.

Mike and Laura's reconnection isn't unusual, but neither is its opposite. Divorce rates among Australians over 50 have risen steadily since 2016, with many separations occurring within five years of the last child leaving home.[1] The empty nest doesn't create relationship problems. It reveals them. However, it also offers an unprecedented opportunity for renewal if couples approach it purposefully.

For some, this begins with small acts of togetherness: setting aside one night a week for a meal at a different spot, planning regular walks or bike rides without phones, or sharing morning coffee before the day pulls you apart. These rituals don't need to be perfectly planned. In fact, the more spontaneous, the better.

Counsellors often notice that couples face three main hurdles during this transition: the loss of shared daily purpose, the rediscovery of fundamental differences, and conflicting needs for closeness versus independence.[2] How you navigate these challenges often determines whether your relationship deepens or deteriorates.

Rekindling shared interests might ease the transition. Revisiting activities you once enjoyed together, such as playing tennis, gardening, or joining a book club, can reignite your curiosity and spark fresh conversations. Even planning a simple weekend getaway without children sharpens the sense of being partners, not just co-parents.

As relationship expert Esther Perel observes, *Most people will have two or three relationships in their lifetime, some with the same person.*[3] The empty nest represents not an ending but a crucial inflection point: a chance to consciously choose each other anew, not as co-parents but as companions for whatever comes next.

Rekindling Physical Connection

The empty nest often coincides with midlife physical changes that affect intimacy. Bodies change, desire shifts, and the easy physical affection that once felt natural may require conscious cultivation. "We had gotten into this pattern of quick kisses goodbye and hurried embraces," reflected Anna, 52. *With the kids gone, we suddenly had privacy but had forgotten how to use it.*

For many couples, rediscovering physical intimacy starts with small, intentional acts of touch: holding hands during evening walks, longer hugs when reuniting at the end of the day, or resting a hand on your partner's shoulder as you pass in the kitchen. You might try couples massage, either professionally guided or by learning gentle techniques at home, to rebuild trust and comfort with touch. Others find closeness through movement rather than stillness. Dancing in the kitchen, joining a beginner's yoga class together, or even trying tai chi in the park can promote playfulness, laughter, and body awareness that ease tension and open new ways to connect.

Simple sensory rituals can also transform the atmosphere. Brewing coffee and sitting close enough for hands to brush across the table, listening to music together in the dark, or lighting a candle at dinner can rekindle presence and attentiveness. Some couples refresh their sleeping space by introducing new sheets, rearranging furniture, or agreeing to keep it free of screens so it feels less like a routine sleep spot and more like a sanctuary for intimacy.

Professional support can be beneficial. Relationship counselling that includes discussing physical intimacy or medical consultation about age-related changes often reassures couples that their experiences are normal and manageable.[4] The key is open communication about what feels good, what has changed, and what new forms of connection might develop.

Just as intimacy needs to be renegotiated, modern family structures also reshape what reconnection looks like. Sophie and Chen, a lesbian couple in Melbourne, channelled their post-nest energy into creating a backyard sanctuary. Planting native grevilleas alongside Chen's grandmother's heritage roses, they cultivated a shared space that reflected their identities. *Working in the soil together*, Sophie laughed. *We talked about things we had never had time for during our teenage years.* Yet intimacy doesn't exist in a vacuum. Broader family responsibilities often intrude just as you might hope for renewal.

The Sandwich Generation

Many empty nesters juggle competing demands, supporting adult children while caring for ageing parents. This squeeze can strain partnerships precisely when couples might hope for more freedom. Susan and Mark from Sydney experienced this when Mark's father developed dementia just as their youngest left for university. Susan recalled finally having their house to themselves, only to find they were managing his father's care, responding to their daughter's university worries, and trying to keep their relationship afloat somewhere in between.

Different approaches to family obligations revealed fundamental differences in their values. Mark felt guilty if they weren't available for every crisis, while Susan felt resentful that his family's needs immediately consumed their newfound freedom. They eventually learned to schedule regular relationship time that couldn't be interrupted by family crises and to have clear, deliberate conversations about their capacity and boundaries.

When extended family demands start to feel over-whelming, it can be helpful to establish dedicated relationship time—such as a weekly dinner, a monthly outing, or even a short overnight getaway. Prioritising time for your part-nership as you would a medical appointment helps prevent caregiving from overshadowing your connection.

Financial pressures often strengthen relationships. David and Jude from Perth set up monthly financial check-ins and structured discussions about family support, retirement plans, and spending priorities. Jude noted that having a regular time to talk about these issues meant they weren't harbouring resentment over smaller daily decisions.

When Distance Reveals Itself

Reconnection isn't inevitable. For some couples, removing parenting pressures exposes fundamental incompatibilities that have obscured shared responsibilities.

Megan experienced this painful realisation when her husband retired and their youngest child moved interstate. *We suddenly found ourselves together all the time, but com-pletely out of sync. I wanted to explore, travel, and talk about our dreams. He retreated to his shed, happy with crosswords and cricket commentary.* After months of gentle efforts to reconnect, they went to counselling with realistic hopes. Sometimes professional guidance reveals a new way forward; other times it shows that loving separation is the kindest choice for both. *It wasn't a failure,* Megan said two years later, living independently and keeping an amicable relationship with her ex-husband. *It was an honest recognition of who we'd become.*

As psychologist Harriet Lerner writes, *A good marriage isn't one where nothing's wrong, but where both partners actively work on what needs attention.*[7] For Megan, that work meant recognising when loving separation was kinder than staying together.

Even in strained relationships, trying new shared activities like volunteering, learning a skill, or travelling can sometimes break long-standing patterns. When seeking professional help, counsellors often encourage couples to create small rituals of connection alongside therapy to see if closeness can be rebuilt. Repair usually starts with the smallest acts for those wanting to rebuild.

Small Steps Toward Repair

Healing strained connections often begins with surprisingly simple gestures. Bronwyn from Adelaide described the awkwardness: *I'd sit opposite him at dinner, wanting to bridge the gap but unsure how to begin.* She and her partner set up a weekly "memory night" sharing old photos over a bottle of wine and reminiscing about their early days in Cairns. These sessions, initially awkward, gradually loosened their emotional distance. Bronwyn explained, *Remembering who we were helped us imagine who we might become.*

Other small practices can be just as effective: keeping a shared journal where each partner writes weekly reflections, choosing a monthly 'surprise date' where one plans something the other enjoys, or setting aside an hour without technology at home. These tools serve as reminders that repair happens through presence, not perfection. The key is to create low-pressure opportunities for genuine connection. Cooking a new recipe together, taking turns choosing weekend activities, or simply asking "What's been on your mind lately?" can reopen channels of intimacy that years of task-focused conversation had narrowed.

Solo Navigation

Partnership is only one thread in the tapestry of empty nest relationships. For those who live alone through choice, circumstance, or loss, the challenges and opportunities look different but no less profound.

For single parents, widowed individuals, or those who've chosen to parent alone, the empty nest presents unique challenges. Your house doesn't just become quiet; it can feel suspended in stillness, without even the rhythm of another adult's presence to mark time. James, a widower in rural Tasmania, felt this acutely after his daughter moved to Hobart. *Every creak of the floorboards seemed amplified*, he recalled. *I'd catch myself listening for sounds that would never come again.*

Single parents often form particularly strong bonds with their children, relationships that serve multiple roles during active parenting years. When children leave, the sense of loss can feel more complete than for couples who still have each other to reconnect with. Practical steps, such as establishing gentle routines, planning regular outings, or fostering rituals of self-care, can bring rhythm in the absence of another adult's presence. You might create weekly 'anchor points,' like a Sunday stroll, a visit to the library, or a call with a friend, that punctuate the week and lessen the feeling of unstructured time.

Yet within the silence, solo empty nesters often uncover unexpected opportunities. You can reimagine your life without having to negotiate another person's preferences. James joined a coastal gardening group that introduced him to people who shared his love of native plants and wry humour. *It wasn't really about the gardens*, he reflected. *It was about feeling part of something alive again.* You might explore creative pursuits long postponed, adopt pets that bring warmth and companionship into the home, or find community through volunteering and interest-based groups. These connections remind solo nesters that although your house may be quiet, life outside its walls remains vibrant and welcoming.

Intentional Connection

This quieter phase of life invites you to approach relationships not from obligation or habit but from genuine curiosity and care. The most significant realisation often emerges gradually: relationships during this stage require the same intentionality that parenting once demanded. Without children's needs providing external structure, you must consciously choose connection, actively nurture intimacy, and deliberately create rituals that honour the people who matter most.

The empty nest isn't the end of relationships but their chance to evolve. Partners can rediscover each other with fresh eyes, solo nesters can strengthen their bonds with themselves and their communities, and adult children can shift from dependence to companionship. Family dynamics might develop into something more genuine and sustainable. Some connections will grow closer, others may loosen, but each change invites us to approach relationships with courage, tenderness, and deliberate choice.

In the opening scene of this chapter, the couple at the table faces an unfamiliar and heavy silence. That silence can remain a burden or become a canvas for renewal. Whether through rekindled intimacy, shared adventures, or a stronger sense of self, the empty nest offers a chance to reimagine how love, loyalty, and connection will look in this new season.

In the next chapter, we will explore how your search for connection extends beyond intimate relationships into broader community and friendship, examining how shared spaces and chosen connections can illuminate this stage of life with renewed purpose and belonging.

Reflections and Practices

Personal Reflection Prompts

- Think about your partnership: what feels newly alive, and what feels strained in this season of life?
- Recall a recent conversation with your adult child. Were you listening to respond, or listening to understand?
- Which relationships in your life feel most nourishing right now? Which feels draining?

Creative Journalling Exercises

- Timeline of Connection: Sketch the journey of your closest relationship from its beginning to now. Where are the strong threads, and where have they frayed?
- Letter Unsent: Write a letter to your partner, adult

child, or sibling expressing what you value about them. You don't need to send it—this is about clarity.

Practical Experiments

- Start a weekly ritual with your partner (a walk, a shared meal, a memory night). Notice what shifts.
- Try asking one open-ended question with an adult child and resisting the urge to advise unless invited.
- Identify one boundary that could improve a relationship—whether with a partner, parent, or child—and test expressing it gently but clearly.

Key Takeaway

The empty nest reshapes every bond. Thriving relationships require intentional curiosity, honest boundaries, and a willingness to meet each other anew.

PART IV:

RECONNECTION AND GROWTH

Chapter 13

Making Friends and Building Community

In the evenings, she found herself wishing for a friend—someone to sit with on a Saturday afternoon, share a glass of wine, and dive into those deep conversations that nourish the soul. She reflected on how much of her life had been devoted to raising children, progressing her career, and managing the endless logistics of family life. Friendships had become afterthoughts, pushed to the margins of busier priorities.

She reached out to old school friends from her own boarding school days and was surprised by how easy it felt to pick up where they'd left off. Little by little, she rebuilt her network, not by waiting, but by reaching out and showing up. She would discover that the answer lay in small acts of courage.

She hadn't set out to build community; it unfolded, one small step at a time. She volunteered as secretary at the local men's shed for several years, offering her time and skills in ways that mattered. She took on the role of editor for a quarterly journal for the Australian Irish Heritage Association, weaving together stories that connected people across distance and generations. She joined the community garden, working the soil alongside neighbours, sharing harvests and conversation.

She sat on a domestic violence committee, contributing quietly but purposefully. And she made a point of showing up at local events, concerts, gatherings, wherever people came together. Reaching out didn't always come easily; sometimes she hesitated to extend invitations and step forward first. But she knew that belonging wasn't just something that arrived. She helped build it piece by piece, showing up, giving, and saying yes.

Connecting With Others

When children's departure changes household dynamics, it transforms your entire social ecosystem. The daily interactions that parenting provided dissolve almost overnight, leaving behind what the 2023 Australian Loneliness Report describes as a "social recession", a subtle but persistent isolation affecting nearly 30% of Australians over 50.[1]

Social confidence, like physical fitness, can atrophy from disuse. You might discover you've become skilled at functional relationships while your capacity for purely personal connections has grown rusty. Yet friendship isn't a luxury. It's essential for both your mental and physical health.

One longitudinal study that tracked individuals' lives for over 80 years consistently demonstrates that good relationships keep us happier and healthier.[2] Other research from Blue Zones regions like Okinawa and Sardinia shows that strong social connections predict longevity better than diet or exercise habits.[3]

Although cultural narratives sometimes suggest that deep friendships belong to youth, the empty nest years offer unique advantages: clarity about your values, freedom from competing demands of small children, and emotional maturity that deepens rather than dramatises relationships. While you can maintain roughly 150 meaningful connections, you typically have space for only five truly close friends, a reminder that quality matters more than quantity.[4]

Understanding why connection matters motivates, but the practical question remains: How do you begin when your social muscles have grown stiff from disuse? Answering that question means starting small and having the gentle courage to try again.

The Art of Beginning Again

Making new friends in midlife requires courage that is different from childhood connections. There's no classroom seating chart or shared dormitory experience to bridge initial awkwardness. Instead, there's vulnerability, the recognition that everyone else might have established social circles while you're starting fresh. This vulnerability often carries unexpected weight. Unlike social anxiety in youth, your midlife friendship fears tap into more profound questions: Have you waited too long? Will anyone find you interesting beyond your family roles?

If you're naturally shy or introverted, this hesitation is entirely usual and nothing to overcome; it's simply your authentic way of approaching new situations. Your goal isn't transformation into someone bold and charismatic; it's finding pathways honouring your natural temperament while creating opportunities for genuine connection.

You might come to see this truth as Julie did when she finally joined the community choir she'd been contemplating for three years. She remembers sitting in the back row for the first six weeks, just listening and barely singing. For her, that felt sufficient. She realised she belonged when she stopped feeling invisible and started harmonising effortlessly. Her approach worked because it honoured her natural personality while placing her in an environment where connection could grow naturally. As Brené Brown suggests, true belonging doesn't mean we have to change who we are; it's about finding our people.[5]

This wisdom points toward a crucial insight: your most sustainable friendships develop not through forced social effort but by consistently placing yourself in environments aligned with your genuine interests. The community often becomes the most natural bridge, allowing friendships to grow without pressure.

Community as the Gateway

The most sustainable path to friendship often involves community involvement rather than direct friend-seeking. When you participate in something larger than social connection alone, relationships develop naturally around shared purpose rather than forced interaction.

Learning Communities

University of the Third Age (U3A) represents one of Australia's most successful models for meaningful midlife connection.[6] With over 250 branches nationwide, U3A offers everything from philosophy discussions to creative writing, photography walks to local history groups. The magic lies in lifelong learning and the natural friendships that emerge when minds engage.

Lucy joined her local U3A's psychology discussion group in Brisbane. She explained that she went because she'd always been curious about human behaviour, but stayed because these people became genuinely interesting to her as individuals. *We'd debate Freud over morning tea, then find ourselves talking about our lives with surprising honesty.*

Creative and Service Communities

Arts-based communities offer rich soil for friendships because creative vulnerability breaks down social barriers. You could take inspiration from Tara, who joined a community garden in Sydney. Conversations over seedling successes and failures connected her with people who gradually became genuine friends. She reflects on how they swapped cuttings and stories, and the loneliness suddenly dissolved.

The Men's and Women's Sheds movements across Australia demonstrate how working with your hands alongside others creates natural camaraderie.[7] The focus on craft or creation provides structure that eases social pressure while building meaningful connections.

Volunteering offers another powerful pathway because shared purpose reduces self-consciousness. Carol, a retired physiotherapist, began watering vegetables weekly at a community garden in Adelaide. She explains that she came to tend the plants but stayed for the morning tea conversations.

Beyond creative and service groups, connections often grow in quieter, less structured ways. Mentoring and teaching are examples. You can share knowledge through a local school reading program, offer career guidance through professional associations, or help coach a junior sports team.

These activities may open doors to friendships with other mentors. The common purpose of supporting the next generation dissolves awkwardness and builds relationships with surprising ease.

Neighbourhood "micro-connections" also hold powerful meaning. A wave to the same dog walker each morning, chats over the fence, or swapping garden produce can feel small, yet these repeated gestures weave threads of belonging. Even weak ties, the familiar faces at the post office or local café, buffer against loneliness and foster your sense of safety. These everyday encounters often become lifelines in rural and remote areas, where formal groups may be scarce. In metro settings, they can puncture anonymity, turning your neighbourhood into a place of recognition.

These structured environments succeed through learning, creating, or serving because they offer natural conversation starters and shared experiences that gradually build familiarity. But what happens when geography or circumstances make traditional community involvement difficult? The answer often now resides online, where digital platforms expand and sometimes even replace the physical community.

Bridges to Real Relationships

Contemporary friendship-building increasingly begins online. Apps like Bumble BFF, Peanut (designed specifically for women seeking platonic relationships), and Meetup have transformed how you find your tribe.[8] These platforms succeed because they enable you to engage gradually, observe before participating, and comment before committing to meetings.

Empty nest support groups, such as those on various social media, offer forums for sharing your experiences with others navigating similar transitions.[9] Digital spaces serve as gateways to your local connections, with online conversations developing into coffee dates and lasting friendships.

Digital platforms also extend into shared learning and play. In a rural area, you can participate in online book clubs, language exchanges, or creative workshops and often find enrichment and friendships that cross state or national borders. As an urban dweller, you can use these platforms to anchor local connections: an online walking group that organises weekend park strolls, or a travel club that begins with photo sharing before meeting at the airport.

Digital platforms can feel exceptionally comfortable if you have an introverted personality because they allow you to engage at your own pace, share thoughts in writing first, and build familiarity before face-to-face meetings.

Addressing Real Barriers

Geographic isolation presents challenges, but digital communities and strategic involvement can bridge gaps. Living outside Broken Hill, Saoirse joined an online watercolour course and built lasting friendships with fellow artists across three states. *We'd share photos of our disasters and breakthroughs*, she laughs, *and the sense of community felt completely real.*

Cultural navigation offers another layer if you're from a migrant or culturally diverse background. After immigrating from Shanghai, Li found community through her local library's multicultural book club. She read about Australian authors with other migrants, which helped her understand the country while staying connected to people who shared the experience of building new lives far from family.

These examples illustrate a key principle: your barriers to connection aren't character flaws to overcome but simply different starting points that require tailored approaches. Your path to friendship will look different from everyone else's, and that's exactly as it should be. Still, whatever your path, lasting friendships are usually built on rhythm and regularity, not one-off encounters.

Sustainable Connections

The most enduring friendships develop through regular interactions rather than sporadic socialising. Heart Foundation Walking Groups operate throughout Australia, offering free environments where shared morning routines foster gradual connection.[10] Penny, sixty-two, joined her local Parkrun on a whim.[11] The events are free, held weekly, and carry no pressure. She describes herself not as a runner but as an enthusiastic walker, often laughing at her own pace as she makes her way around the course. But the post-run coffee chats became the highlight of her week. After six months, she'd built genuine friendships with three women who, like her, had realised that consistency matters more than speed.

These groups succeed because they prioritise regularity over performance. Your presence becomes familiar, creating safety that allows relationships to emerge. Sometimes friendships develop through simple gestures: offering transport to events, suggesting coffee after regular activities, or being genuinely curious about others' experiences. Your transition from activity partner to friend often happens gradually, through accumulated small interactions that build trust and reveal compatibility. Your connection isn't necessarily about intimacy but belonging to something bigger than yourself.

Belonging to Something Larger

The most accessible connections exist through inclusive events and activities in your immediate community. Local festivals, farmers' markets, cultural celebrations, and neighbourhood gatherings offer opportunities to feel part of something larger than individual social needs. These spaces ask nothing of you except presence, yet they weave you into the fabric of your surroundings simply by showing up.

Belonging often grows most naturally from joy and play rather than serious intent. Dance classes, cycling groups, or board game nights create bonds without the weight of expectation. Laughter and lightness make the connection feel effortless rather than engineered. Similarly, spiritual or reflective communities can offer this sense of belonging through traditional faith spaces, meditation circles, yoga studios, or grief support gatherings. These communities provide ritual and rhythm that anchor you in something meaningful, creating opportunities for deeper friendships and gentle companionship that doesn't demand constant engagement.

Caregiving roles also weave you into communities in unexpected ways. If you're a grandparent at the sidelines of sports games, a carer who meets others during aged-care visits, or a parent rotating school pickups, you naturally form support networks. The bond isn't forced friendship but shared responsibility, a common understanding that frequently ripens into genuine camaraderie. Intergenerational connections often develop naturally in these shared spaces, much like community choirs or volunteer organisations, where age becomes less relevant than shared purpose. These relationships carry less social pressure and allow for natural generosity, creating bonds that enrich everyone. With so many possible avenues, the key is to move at a natural pace.

Your Natural Pace

Building friendships in midlife requires patience with yourself and others and the natural development of trust. Not every coffee date will become a lasting friendship, and not every group immediately feels like home. This variation is entirely normal.

If you're naturally introverted, honour that tendency. You might find a connection by sitting quietly at the back of classes, absorbing the atmosphere before participating. You might prefer side-by-side activities over face-to-face intensity, or behind-the-scenes volunteer roles that provide natural conversation starters. There's no single right way to connect. Research from Relationships Australia reveals that Australians increasingly prioritise quality over quantity in social connections, seeking nourishing and sincere relationships rather than performative ones.[12]

The relationships you build become both foundation and inspiration for more profound questions about purpose and contribution. How do you want to shape this next season? What difference do you want to make? The next chapter will explore these questions through the lens of career, creativity, and meaningful contribution.

Reflections and Practices
Personal Reflection Prompts
1. When you imagine ideal friendship in this stage of life, what qualities or experiences matter most?
2. Think of one past friendship that brought you joy. What can you learn from that experience for how you want to connect now?
3. What fears or hesitations surface when you consider making new friends? How might you respond to them with kindness?

Creative Journalling Exercises
- Mapping Connection: Draw a simple map of your social world—family, colleagues, acquaintances, neighbours. Where are the gaps? Where might new friendships take root?
- Future Letter: Write a short letter to your "future friend"—the person you haven't met yet but hope to. What would you tell them about yourself?

Practical Experiments
- Join one community group, class, or volunteer opportunity that aligns with a genuine interest, and commit to attending for at least four weeks.
- Reach out to one acquaintance with a simple invitation—a walk, a coffee, or a phone call.
- Try a "micro-connection": a short conversation with someone at the local shop, park, or market. These small acts often build confidence for deeper steps.

Key Takeaway

Friendship and community in the empty nest years are not luxuries but lifelines, built through small acts of courage, consistency, and authentic presence.

Chapter 14

Career and Purpose in the Empty Nest Years

*S*he hadn't expected to feel so hungry for a challenge for something that didn't have a name yet. She hadn't planned it, but learning always found her. She had built her career one qualification at a time: a Bachelor of Arts, then Literature and Communication, then a Graduate Diploma, a Master's, and finally a Doctorate. She taught literacy to teenagers, computing to seniors, language to migrant women, multimedia to First Nation people, and confidence to women who'd never been told they deserved it. She travelled across the state, running mental health first aid workshops in far-flung towns. Each class and each centre felt like a small offering, where learning could be reclaimed, no matter how late in life it arrived. Teaching became more than a job. It was how she stitched herself back together.

Outside of work, she enrolled in online courses, mostly free, following her curiosity wherever it led. She explored art classes, editing courses, and publishing workshops. She watched YouTube tutorials to try new art techniques, experimented with various materials, and always sought to discover what else she could create. She began selling her artwork. Even *after leaving formal employment, she continued learning, subscribing to journals, and staying connected. She continued her voluntary role as editor of a quarterly heritage journal, utilising her skills in new ways. For her, learning wasn't about qualifications anymore but staying engaged, interested, and alive to possibilities.*

In seeking purpose, she's called to adapt, to learn new tools, speak new languages, and stay connected in an increasingly online world. The hunger that surprised her became not a burden but a compass, pointing her toward the next life she could claim as her own.

Why Now?

The empty nest years arrive at a unique convergence of circumstances that make career reinvention not just possible, but almost inevitable. For the first time in decades, your time is essentially your own.

It's more than just having time. This phase offers you emotional clarity that wasn't present during the intensity of active parenting. You understand yourself better—what energises and drains you, which values truly matter, and which compromises you're willing to accept. Financial necessity, geographic constraints, or family logistics often influenced your career choices in your twenties and thirties. Now, you can select based on meaning, interest, and personal fulfilment.

The modern economy has shifted dramatically in your favour. Remote work has grown from a workplace perk to a standard option across many industries.[1] The gig economy provides flexible, project-based work that fits around other life commitments. Online education has made high-quality learning accessible from your kitchen table.[2] Digital platforms allow you to start a side hustle or small business with minimal startup costs.

Perhaps most importantly, society's attitude towards traditional career paths has shifted. The expectation of working for one employer for thirty years has vanished. Career pivots are now standard, even expected. Age diversity in workplaces is increasingly seen as valuable rather than burdensome. Research from the Australian Human Rights Commission confirms that mature workers bring essential skills, including emotional intelligence, reliability, and institutional knowledge that younger colleagues often lack.[3] Your decades of life experience offer wisdom, emotional intelligence, and hard-won perspective.

The Emotional Landscape of Starting Again

Recognising opportunity doesn't automatically eliminate the complex emotions accompanying significant life changes. Your prospect of career reinvention may trigger some anxiety, even when you feel ready for something new.

After years of focusing on others' development, you might discover your professional confidence has eroded. Your skills feel rusty. Industries have evolved beyond recognition. Technology that seemed manageable five years ago now feels intimidating. This isn't imaginary. It reflects fundamental gaps that need addressing. But it's also more surmountable than it initially appears. You might relate to Rose, who experienced this acutely when considering a return to marketing after eight years of part-time consulting. *I felt like Rip Van Winkle, she laughed, waking up to discover social media marketing had become a whole profession while I was focused on school fundraisers.*

Rather than diving immediately into job applications, Rose spent three months slowly rebuilding her confidence. She took an online course in digital marketing, updated her LinkedIn profile, and began following industry discussions online. She figured, *I didn't need to become an expert; I just needed to become conversant enough to contribute meaningfully.*

The key insight is that you don't need to close every skill gap before starting. You need to close enough gaps to participate confidently, then learn the rest while doing it. Confidence gaps are part of the challenge. You might question whether your experience still matters. You could struggle with deeper questions about whether your experience remains valuable in rapidly changing work environments. This concern feels especially strong in technology-related sectors, but it extends beyond digital skills to include broader issues around workplace culture, communication styles, and professional expectations. These doubts often conceal a more basic fear: that the professional world has forgotten you, that your years of focusing on family have made you invisible or irrelevant to potential employers or clients.

The opposite is often true. The skills you've developed over years of managing family logistics, coordinating community events, leading school committees, and organising local fundraisers easily transfer to professional settings. Project management, conflict resolution, budget oversight, volunteer coordination, and stakeholder engagement are exactly the abilities modern workplaces seek. If you're a rural woman, you often possess outstanding relationship-building and problem-solving skills gained through necessity in smaller communities where teamwork and resourcefulness are crucial.

The opposite is often true. The skills you've sharpened through years of managing family logistics, organising community events, leading school committees, and funding local projects transfer directly to professional settings. In rural communities, where formal services may be limited and teamwork becomes vital, you often develop outstanding relationship-building and problem-solving skills through necessity.[4] Project management, conflict resolution, budget oversight, volunteer coordination, and stakeholder engagement are precisely the skills modern workplaces value.[5] Whether you've been stretching resources over large distances, building networks in smaller populations, or juggling multiple roles because specialists aren't always available, these experiences foster resourcefulness and adaptability that urban professionals may take years to develop. The creative problem-solving needed when outsourcing isn't an option, or calling in an expert builds a broad and resilient professional foundation.

Real Barriers, Real Solutions

Acknowledging the emotional complexity of career reinvention means honestly confronting the systemic barriers that make it genuinely challenging, not just personally difficult. Real solutions to these barriers exist, from ageism to financial risks to geographic constraints and opportunities.

Age discrimination in hiring remains a persistent reality, with studies showing that applications from workers over 45 receive fewer callbacks than identical applications from younger candidates.[6] You might feel dismissed during job interviews, with your experience characterised as "overqualified," or sense that younger hiring managers view you as less adaptable or technologically capable.

These experiences are not paranoia, but reflections of genuine bias.[7] Overcoming them requires your strategy rather than wishful thinking. One practical approach is to target companies that actively demonstrate age diversity in their leadership and recruitment. Another is to emphasise recent skills and continuous learning instead of relying on lengthy career histories that employers may skim over. Networking through professional connections often proves more effective than submitting cold applications through online portals. Contract or project-based work might provide a practical way to showcase abilities before a formal hiring decision is made. Your goal is not to hide years of experience, but to frame it in ways that address potential concerns about adaptability and up-to-date knowledge.

Career reinvention carries financial risks that vary by circumstance.

Financial issues often extend beyond simple income calculations when you live in areas where property assets may be substantial but cash savings are limited. You might encounter higher costs for professional development due to travel requirements and a lack of access to specialised financial advisers familiar with regional economic patterns. The seasonal nature of many regional industries can make a steady alternative income particularly vital, yet geographical isolation can limit local opportunities.

These concerns warrant your serious consideration. A sensible initial step is to secure transition funding through current employment or gradual skill development rather than rushing into something entirely new. Starting with low-risk experiments, such as freelance work or part-time roles, allows you to test the waters before committing to significant changes. Professional financial advice can be invaluable, ensuring career shifts do not threaten your retirement security while enabling you to explore location-specific opportunities like land-based businesses or regional development grants.

If you live outside major cities, you face unique and additional challenges in career reinvention. Limited local employment options may mean you need to consider remote work, starting a business, or accepting longer commutes. Professional development courses often require travel to regional centres, adding time and cost barriers.[8] Yet, your location offers distinct advantages: lower business startup costs, strong community support networks, and opportunities to serve underserved markets where your understanding of local needs becomes a competitive advantage.

The rise of remote work has been particularly transformative for women in regional areas. After 25 years in a remote northwest mining town, Helen began teaching part-time at the local TAFE, helping adults improve their literacy and digital skills. Her deep understanding of regional challenges made her especially effective and fulfilled. She reflects that it wasn't about reclaiming my old career but stepping into something new with all the wisdom I'd gained. Online platforms allowed her to supplement local teaching with virtual tutoring clients nationwide, dramatically expanding her potential market without relocating.

Pathways to Reinvention

Career reinvention in midlife rarely follows a single template. Most successful transitions emerge through experimentation, testing different approaches until you find the path that fits your circumstances, interests, and goals. That means stepping back into classrooms and courses or launching a business or creative venture.[9] You might begin with a side hustle that grows unexpectedly or choose the stability of returning to traditional work. Each offers opportunities, challenges, and rewards, creating a broad choice landscape.

The Learning Path

Formal and informal learning are two of the most common pathways available. Many women return to study, discovering that structured education provides the skills and confidence needed for new career directions. For some, this means pursuing formal qualifications through TAFE, universities, or professional certifications. At 64, Jan, from regional New South Wales, completed an Individual Support certificate through TAFE and now works part-time in aged care. She explained that she wanted meaningful work, and the course gave her the skills and confidence to enter a new field.

You might focus on skill-specific training. Short courses in digital marketing, project management, bookkeeping, or creative fields often provide faster entry into employment or self-employment. You could follow your curiosity into interest-led exploration. A pottery class or photography workshop you begin for personal enrichment may gradually evolve into teaching, selling, or offering creative services. The great advantage of the learning pathway is that it allows you to explore interests while building capabilities. It provides a low-pressure environment where confidence can develop gradually, making your transition into a new field less intimidating and more sustainable.

The Entrepreneurial Path

Starting your own venture, whether a traditional business, consulting practice, or creative enterprise, offers maximum flexibility and control over your work environment. Modern technology has dramatically lowered the barriers to entrepreneurship, enabling you to start and test ideas with minimal upfront investment.

One option is to create a service-based business. Consulting, coaching, tutoring, or other professional services allow you to build on your expertise. These ventures often require very little startup capital yet benefit significantly from your accumulated experience and existing networks.

Another option is to explore online businesses. E-commerce shops, digital courses, content creation, or online services can reach customers beyond your local area. With platforms like Etsy, Teachable, or Shopify, you can now access infrastructure that previously cost thousands to develop. You might also consider a local venture. Businesses that serve your immediate community, such as catering, pet services, home organising, or specialised retail, can be very successful. These kinds of enterprises often thrive because of your local knowledge and the trust you've built through community connections.

The Side Hustle Strategy

Not every career reinvention requires you to leave your current job or make major life shifts. You can effectively develop side hustles: income-generating activities that eventually become full-time careers or remain rewarding supplements to other work. Side hustles are especially useful when juggling multiple commitments because they let you experiment without risking too much financially. You can scale them up or down depending on life's circumstances, providing flexibility when family or community needs change.

They also provide extra sources of income that reduce financial stress and encourage independence. Side hustles often develop naturally from your existing interests or skills, making them a rewarding extension of what you already enjoy. Examples include freelance writing, online tutoring, handmade crafts, photography services, virtual assistance, or specialised consulting. The key is to start with something manageable that suits your current abilities while allowing room for growth.

Melissa and her daughter, Grace, started thinking about selling clothing online during a long harvest season on their mixed-farming property. They had always loved fashion but lived hours from the nearest boutique. What began as a few weekend listings of expressive, comfortable pieces like linen shirts, relaxed skirts, and rural-chic accessories quickly gained momentum. Using their farmhouse kitchen table as an office and the machinery shed as a stockroom, they launched an online store.

For Melissa, the experience rekindled a sense of creative purpose that farming alone couldn't offer. For Grace, it became a way to develop business skills and digital marketing without leaving home. Together, they demonstrated that innovation could thrive in unexpected places. This modern side hustle turned a local idea into a national success story, even on a remote property.

The Return-to-Work Path

After years of limited workforce participation, you might return to traditional employment. This route provides stability and structure but demands careful management of the challenges of such a transition.

A triumphant return often starts by updating skills through short courses or online learning. This helps rebuild confidence and demonstrates adaptability to potential employers. Consider returning to work through temporary, contract, or part-time roles. These options allow you and the employer to evaluate compatibility before committing long-term. Targeting organisations known for valuing diverse experience and age inclusion also boosts your chances of a triumphant return. Support makes your journey more sustainable, no matter which path you choose.

Building Your Support Network

Career reinvention rarely succeeds in isolation. Building supportive networks becomes crucial for maintaining momentum, accessing opportunities, and navigating inevitable challenges. Professional networks can open crucial doors. Industry associations, LinkedIn groups, or local business organisations give you access to job opportunities, current trends, and professional growth. These connections often hold more value than formal applications for finding and securing opportunities.

Peer support groups also play an essential role. Connecting with other women experiencing similar transitions provides emotional encouragement and practical advice. These groups might be formal, such as those offered through organisations like Business Chicks, or they may develop more informally through courses, workshops, or community activities. Mentorship relationships add another layer of strength to your journey. Seeking mentors who share guidance and experience can accelerate your development, while offering mentorship to younger professionals allows you to contribute to others' success and build confidence in your path.

Family support is just as important. Honest conversations with family members about your goals, time commitments, and changing roles help build the support you need for a successful transition. This might involve renegotiating household responsibilities or setting clear expectations about your availability, ensuring your reinvention has a strong foundation.

Starting Where You Are

Career reinvention doesn't need a dramatic performance or perfect planning. It starts with an honest review of where you are now, clear thoughts about what you want to change, and small trial steps towards those changes. The process might begin by identifying activities or topics that consistently catch your interest, then evaluating skills gained through volunteering, parenting, or community involvement that might translate into new directions. Researching one field or opportunity that intrigues you, without any commitment to pursue it, can open unexpected pathways. Connecting with one person whose career path interests you or taking a course related to a potential interest creates momentum without pressure. Attending an event in an unfamiliar field might reveal possibilities you hadn't considered. The aim isn't to have everything figured out before starting, but to begin moving in a promising direction while staying open to unexpected opportunities that emerge along the way.

You're not starting from scratch. You're building on decades of your experience, wisdom, and capabilities, which are valuable in today's economy. Consider what form your reinvention will take and how quickly you want to move toward it. The empty nest years present a rare opportunity for time, experience, and chance to come together. They invite you to engage in work, study, or projects that are no longer driven by the demands of raising children but by your values, energy, and interests. The obstacles are real, but so are the resources, networks, and inner strengths that can support you.

Your ability to stay connected becomes an integral part of this journey as your ambitions evolve, whether gradually or with bold ambition. Pursuing purpose increasingly requires digital confidence to access opportunities, connect with networks, and reach broader markets. The next chapter will explore how mastering these tools can transform your career prospects and your entire approach to learning, creativity, and staying engaged with the world around you.

Reflections and Practices

Individual Reflection Prompts

- What activities or tasks make you lose track of time? What do they suggest about where your energy naturally flows?
- What career or learning dream did you set aside when you were younger? Does it still hold meaning for you now?
- When you imagine yourself five years from now, what role or purpose do you most want to be claiming?

Creative Journalling Exercises

The Career Timeline

Draw a timeline of your working life so far. Mark the roles you've had (paid and unpaid), the skills you've gained, and the moments of pride or joy. Then add a "future stretch" line projecting three roles or projects you'd like to explore next.

The Curiosity List

Write down 15 things you're curious about, from pottery to coding to politics. Circle three that spark the most excitement. What's one small step you could take toward exploring each?

Ongoing Check-Ins

- What did I learn this week that stretched me beyond my comfort zone?
- Which activities left me energised, and which drained me?
- Did I take one small step toward a career, project, or learning goal?

Key Takeaway

Career reinvention in the empty nest years is not about starting over but transforming lived experience, curiosity, and resilience into meaningful new opportunities.

Chapter 15

A Guide to Staying Connected

*S*he thought she was being clever, downloading TikTok the *moment it became the next big thing. Within hours, she enthusiastically shared what she thought were hilarious cat videos with her daughters, only to be gently informed that she'd likely fallen for a scam. The irony was delicious; here was a woman who'd spent years patiently teaching other older adults how to navigate computers, helping them send their first emails and fumble through video calls with grandchildren. Yet her daughters looked at her like she needed training wheels.*

That's precisely where you find yourself during these empty nest years. When you believe you've got one thing sorted, the landscape shifts beneath your feet. Apps change overnight, new platforms pop up like mushrooms after rain, and suddenly you're asking for help instead of giving it. Keeping up with technology isn't about being trendy or cool; it's about survival. It's about staying connected, curious, and, most importantly, independent when everything else seems to be changing.

This isn't a chapter teaching you to become a tech guru or impress anyone with your digital skills. It's about recognising that technology has quietly become the gateway to almost everything you need: healthcare, banking, staying connected with loved ones, and even basic services you used to take for granted. We will explore why digital literacy has shifted from *nice to have* to *essential* and how embracing it can turn your potential isolation into genuine empowerment.

When the World Goes Digital

You might find yourself in this situation, like Mabel did at 62, not because she wanted to, but because she had no choice.

For years, Mabel had been content letting her daughter handle all the computer-related tasks that seemed too complicated to learn. Then her doctor's office announced that phone appointments were no longer available and everything had to be booked online. The announcement triggered panic and the fear of permanent dependence on her daughter. But her daughter had moved interstate for work, leaving Mabel to manage on her own. She enrolled in a library technology class, became the slowest learner in the room, and laughed through her struggles while practising on her tablet every evening. Six months later, she booked appointments, video-called specialists, and managed prescriptions online. The realisation came that avoiding technology hadn't protected her independence but had been giving it away.

Her experience has become universal. The digital divide isn't just about convenience anymore; it's about access to the basic infrastructure of modern life. Healthcare systems have embraced patient portals and telehealth appointments.[1] Banks are shutting branches.[2] Government services, pension management, and grocery deliveries now assume comfort with navigating websites, downloading apps, and managing passwords.[3]

This vast change occurred during the empty nest years, when the tech-savvy kids moved out, leaving you to figure things out independently. Your temptation to hand it all over to someone else is strong, but that leads straight to dependence, the opposite of the hard-won independence you've built over decades.

As more institutions go digital-only, your ability to log in, verify your identity, complete transactions, and navigate basic online systems becomes as essential as knowing how to drive. Women who adopt this early often find it liberating; suddenly, you can organise your schedule, make appointments, and handle business without coordinating with anyone else or sitting on hold for forty-five minutes. And when access moves online, choosing not to participate has its consequences.

The Real Cost of Stepping Back

The cost of avoiding digital engagement adds up quickly and can be severe. Healthcare demonstrates this clearly. Telehealth appointments tripled in 2024 and show no signs of slowing down. Prescription refills, test results, and specialist consultations all require some level of app navigation or online portal management. Without these skills, you're stuck on endless hold, risking missed medical updates, or worse, delayed treatments because you couldn't access your results or book follow-up appointments. Your financial independence takes a similar hit as banks push everything online,[4] and MyGov handles Medicare, Centrelink payments, and tax affairs.[5]

But perhaps the most painful cost is social. Your connections increasingly shift to digital channels. Your grandchildren share milestones on Instagram, friends arrange catch-ups through Facebook groups, and families stay connected via messaging threads. Without your engagement in these spaces, you're not just missing convenience, you're missing life itself.

The world isn't pausing for your digital hesitation, but here's some good news: it's more accessible than ever for those willing to try it. Yet the same tools that seem necessary to you can turn into surprisingly gentle bridges.

From Necessity to Something Beautiful

You might never have seen yourself as tech-savvy. Jane, at 64, wasn't about to start now, but when her daughter moved to London, the answer was clear: master video calls or let the relationship drift apart. Sunday mornings are sacred for Rita as she settles in with her tea and laptop, her daughter's face brightening the screen from her tiny London flat.

Rita admits, *It's not the same as having her here in person, but seeing her face and watching her make that terrible coffee she's so proud of, reminds me she's still mine, just living her life elsewhere..*

This happens when you see technology not as a barrier to overcome but as a bridge to connect. Video calls create real presence across continents. Your first attempt might only show your forehead, but you'll laugh about it together, and the next call will feel more natural. These small rituals often become the most treasured parts of your week.

Messaging apps act like modern letterboxes for quick

texts, photos, and shared moments. Family group chats become digital hearths where different generations swap news and terrible jokes in real time. Social media offers windows into adult children's worlds; a simple like on their post holds more emotional weight than expected.

The key is to begin with one genuine connection rather than trying to master everything simultaneously. Pick the family member you most want to stay close to, choose one method that appeals to you, and focus on that until it feels natural. Connection doesn't end at the family thread; it broadens when you find your people.

Finding Your People Beyond Family

Digital spaces are more than communication tools. They are gathering places for shared interests that can transform the empty nest isolation into growth and genuine friendship. Your secret is finding one authentic community around something you care about and letting that passion motivate your learning.

Janine, 59, from Perth, joined a Facebook journaling group during lockdown almost as an experiment. *I thought it would be a few writing prompts she remembers. Instead, I found women dealing with precisely what I was: kids gone, careers winding down, wondering what comes next.* Three years later, she developed real friendships across Australia and participated in virtual writing retreats. When her group organised a Perth meetup, eight women supporting each other through screens finally shared coffee and stories in person.

These communities share ideas, host live tutorials and organise challenges across different time zones. Virtual friendships might lead to in-person meetups or remain wonderfully online. There's flexibility for mobility issues, budget constraints, or simple preferences. The beauty is finding your tribe first, then letting the technology follow naturally. Once you've found a community that genuinely resonates with you, your motivation to develop digital confidence naturally grows. That's because you're no longer just learning technology for its own sake but to strengthen connections that already matter to you.

Building Confidence in Small Steps

Building digital confidence works like any other skill. It requires patience, practice, and the freedom to make mistakes without fear of judgment. Programs such as Australia's Be Connected and Tech Savvy Seniors offer free training tailored for adult learners. Libraries and community centres run workshops where instructors recognise that participants bring valuable life experience to their learning. It is worth exploring what is available.

For those living in regional areas, these challenges add extra complexity. Elena, aged sixty-seven from rural Victoria, learned smartphone banking after her local bank branch shut, saving herself two-hour drives to town. The closure of local services often speeds up the need to go digital in ways that city dwellers don't experience as acutely. She reflected that she once thought she was too old to learn new tricks and realised she had only been scared of trying something unfamiliar. Once she allowed herself to give it a go, she found it wasn't nearly as tricky as she'd thought.

The closure of bank branches, post offices, and service

centres makes digital literacy especially important for rural women. Limited internet access can make learning difficult, but mobile data and better regional infrastructure are slowly bridging these gaps. The independence gained often surpasses the initial difficulties. Over time, it becomes easier to manage banking, book medical appointments, and access government services without long trips to town or relying on others.

For self-paced learning, YouTube tutorials allow you to pause, rewind, and replay until concepts make sense. Ten minutes a day can turn uncertainty into basic competence surprisingly quickly. These new skills often open doors you did not know existed.

Mel, a retired nurse from regional Western Australia, learned Canva during lockdown and now designs promotional materials for local cafes, turning her new skills into contribution and income. Lyn, aged sixty-two, took her first pottery class on a whim. What began as a simple hobby, something to do with her hands now that she was no longer packing school lunches, grew into a small business from her backyard studio. Three years later, she sells her pieces through Instagram to customers across Australia. She had never imagined herself as an entrepreneur but followed her curiosity and discovered it could lead to something fulfilling.

The key is to start small and celebrate every achievement. Whether booking an appointment online or joining a video call, each accomplishment builds confidence for the next challenge. Skill grows with practice, and courage grows each time you face a fear.

Getting Past the Fear Factor

The fear of making mistakes often masks deeper concerns about competence, but here's the truth: every online booking you complete and video call you manage builds your confidence and independence. Try acknowledging the fear rather than pretending it doesn't exist.

Your safety concerns are valid; scams have become sophisticated,[10] but strong passwords (unique phrases with numbers and symbols), two-factor authentication (where your phone receives a code to confirm it's you), and sticking to trusted websites provide solid protection.[11] A simple rule: if an email asks you to "click here immediately" or threatens account closure unless you act right now, it's almost certainly a scam. Legitimate organisations give you time to respond and provide multiple ways to contact them directly.

Learning these basics protects your information and helps you navigate online spaces with confidence. Most of your worries fade as you become familiar; what seems impossible on day one turns into routine after weeks of steady practice. And now, a new helper has entered the chat: AI. It can feel both awe-inspiring and daunting at first, but it has the power to make even the trickiest digital tasks easier than you might think. With patience and practice, it becomes less of a mystery and more of a practical, everyday assistant.

Your New AI Companion

Remember Mabel, struggling with her doctor's patient portal? Here's where artificial intelligence is truly transforming things: making technology more accessible by removing the biggest hurdles you face. Unlike traditional systems that require precise navigation, AI tools understand your natural language. They respond to questions asked as simply and naturally as everyday chat. This turns intimidating health-care portals, banking websites, and government forms from barriers into manageable tasks.

Mabel now uses AI to decode medical terminology before appointments. She says *I paste the confusing parts into an app and ask it to explain in plain English. Then I can focus on my health instead of feeling overwhelmed by the technology.* She uses it to organise symptoms before telehealth calls and even rehearse difficult conversations with her doctor.

Rita, who learned to use video calls to stay connected with her daughter in London, now uses AI to help her in composing thoughtful emails and organising digital photos before sharing them. The AI doesn't replace her connection; it simply helps her prepare for richer conversations and handle the technical aspects that used to be barriers. The beauty of AI is its endless patience with repeated questions and its ability to break down complex tasks into simple steps. Voice-enabled versions support those with vision or mobility issues, making technology more inclusive than ever.

While AI is helpful, it's not perfect. It can sometimes misunderstand your requests or give outdated information. Think of it as a helpful assistant, not a substitute for professional advice, especially medical or financial advice. Also, be cautious about sharing sensitive personal details; avoid pasting bank account numbers, Medicare details, or other private data into AI tools without checking their privacy policies and security measures. Once the basics are manageable, technology can help extend your voice without taking over your life.

Technology for Civic Life and Balance

Digital skills don't just connect you to family and friends; they can also strengthen your voice in your community. Platforms like Change.org enable you to support causes you care about.[13] Community groups assist in organising local initiatives, from neighbourhood clean-ups to helping local businesses.

Linda, 62, from regional Queensland, used these tools to organise community support networks after her kids left home, channelling her empty nest energy into meaningful local impact. What began as a simple Facebook group to coordinate meal deliveries for elderly neighbours evolved into a broader network connecting isolated residents with volunteers, arranging transport for medical appointments, and maintaining communication that would have been hard to coordinate face-to-face. These platforms turn your individual passion into collective action, allowing you to create real change from your kitchen table.

Technology's promise is choice, not constant connectivity. Setting boundaries is essential: designating tech-free times, turning off notifications during meals, and choosing which platforms deserve your attention. Your goal is mindful engagement that supports your well-being rather than mindless scrolling that drains it. Platforms will evolve, apps will come and go, but the core idea remains. Pick one tool that supports your connection goals and builds confidence before trying others. With boundaries set, your horizons will expand.

Looking Ahead

You don't need to master every app or keep pace with every innovation. Instead, identify what supports your idea of a connected, independent, and engaged life, and confidently ignore the rest. Stories like Mabel's healthcare independence and Rita's ocean-spanning Sunday calls show that technology supports, not replaces, human connection. You don't need expertise; you need access. It's about your conscious involvement in a growing digital world, building confidence through creativity and contribution.

Technology places the world at your fingertips, but sometimes, you want to step into it. The next stage of the empty nest journey explores a different connection: the desire to discover new places. Whether it's solo travel, ancestral journeys, or weekend getaways, digital skills will be vital for planning adventures and rediscovering the world on your terms.

Reflections and Practices

Guided Writing Exercises

The First Step Plan: Write down one digital task you've been avoiding, like setting up online banking or learning a new app. Break it into three simple steps. Commit to completing the first one this week.

- Letters You'll Never Send: Write a short note to your children or grandchildren, describing how it feels to be learning digital tools at this stage of life. Be honest about your fears, frustrations, and victories.

Challenge for the Hesitant

If you've been avoiding digital skills because "it's too late" or "too complicated, " set yourself this one-week challenge:

- Day 1: Ask someone younger to show you one feature on your phone or laptop you've never used.
- Day 3: Practise that feature independently—repeat until you feel comfortable.
- Day 5: Use it for something meaningful (send a voice note, book an appointment, share a photo).
- Day 7: Reflect—did it feel easier than you expected? What new possibilities opened up?

Key Takeaway

Digital literacy in the empty nest years isn't about keeping up with every trend—it's about choosing the tools that keep you connected, independent, and empowered. One small digital step at a time can open doors to richer relationships, smoother daily life, and a future where you remain confident and engaged.

Chapter 16

Travel: Exploring New Places

W*hen seeding finished, she sat by the fireplace in her cold farmhouse and bought a ticket to somewhere she had never been. On another occasion, she booked a weekend getaway to a garden festival, and another to a country motel. Sometimes she camped at local rock formations with a thermos and a book. Travel didn't need to be wildly adventurous to be transformative. Each small adventure reminded her that the world was still vast, still brimming with possibility, and she was free to explore it on her terms. She had travelled extensively since the kids left home. Sometimes she went solo, wandering the streets of Ireland or exploring Indonesian islands nearby. She frequently travelled with her partner, booking river cruises through Europe, supporting her daughter as she raced through the mountains around Chamonix, or wandering along trails in France and Spain's solar farms and citrus orchards. She ventured into Morocco, the USA, Central America, Asia, and Vietnam.*

Each journey taught her something about humanity: people are remarkably alike despite their different languages, customs, and landscapes. She saw the same hopes for peace, freedom, and connection everywhere she went. Travel stretched her, challenged her, and delighted her. And yet, recalling Alain de Botton's message in The Art of Travel, she always returned home to the same self.[1] *Travel wasn't an escape from her identity but an invitation to see the world and herself more clearly and compassionately.*

New Places

You stand at the departure gate, passport in hand, wondering if you want to travel alone at your age. Your friends looked concerned when you announced your plans: a month-long trip through Southeast Asia, or better still, South America, something you'd always dreamed of but never found time for. What surprises you isn't fear. It's pure excitement. You're about to do something entirely for yourself for the first time in decades.

The empty nest can be your ticket to anywhere. With the kids grown and daily chores eased, this stage offers the chance to explore new places and discover different versions of yourself. Travel shifts from being just an escape to a way of finding out who you might become.

As Alain de Botton reminds us, we don't just visit places; places also visit us, altering how we perceive ourselves and our everyday world. Returning from wandering Irish coastlines, you'll see your garden differently. Navigating Tokyo's subway system reveals your own quiet competence, and drifting along the Mekong River may leave you attuned to the steady pulse of movement and stillness. Travel doesn't need crossing oceans to be transformative; it only requires crossing the threshold of routine.

However, you might not feel ready to book that international adventure. After years of financial sacrifice, health concerns, or confidence knocked by major life transitions, travel can feel like watching someone else's highlight reel. The fear isn't always about destinations. It's about feeling you deserve them. You might worry you're too old, unfit, or in-experienced to travel far. You might also worry about feeling out of place among younger travellers, handling unfamiliar systems alone, or dealing with physical limits in foreign en-vironments. These worries are real and valid, but they don't have to be lifelong barriers.

The Psychology of Elsewhere

Why does the idea of "somewhere else" hold such sway during life changes? It's because familiar surroundings reflect who you've been, while unfamiliar places invite you to explore who you might become. In your own kitchen, you're the person who always burns the toast. In a Tuscan cooking class, you might discover an intuitive understanding of flavour you never knew you had.

The excitement you feel exploring maps, learning about customs, and imagining chats with strangers starts to change you even before you leave home. This preparatory dreaming isn't silly; it's your mind practising flexibility, rehearsing courage, and expanding its view of what's possible. Even the smallest break from routine can shift your outlook. Book a night at a local country inn, and you'll come home seeing your town with tourist eyes, noticing details that had faded into the background. This pull toward "elsewhere" doesn't always mean crossing oceans. Often, your first steps into reinvention begin in your own backyard.

Day Adventures and Local Discovery

Your most meaningful journeys sometimes happen closest to home. Your area probably holds landscapes and experiences you've never truly explored: scenic spots you've only driven through, cultural sites you've always intended to visit, or lively neighbourhoods you've never found the time to discover. Becoming a tourist in familiar areas often uncovers hidden gems. Visit that regional gallery you've driven past for years, and you might find a new passion for contemporary art. Book a country railway trip through landscapes you know only from car windows.

Local-themed adventures offer focus without needing passports, such as wellness weekends at regional spas, food and wine journeys through nearby districts, and arts and culture immersions via local performances and exhibitions. These experiences show that meaningful discovery doesn't require international travel, just an openness to viewing familiar places with fresh curiosity. When seen through a traveller's eyes, your city can become a source of wonder. That museum you've never visited, the neighbourhood you've only driven past, and the restaurant everyone talks about often need little planning but provide great renewal.

Meaningful travel doesn't always mean crossing oceans. Australia's backyard offers wonders as captivating as any overseas destination, from desert blooms in the Red Centre to stunning coastlines along Tasmania's edges. The phenomenon of "grey nomads" embracing mobile lifestyles shows a growing realisation that adventure is everywhere if you want to seek it out. The country's popular touring routes, such as the Great Ocean Road, the Nullarbor crossing, and circuits through the Kimberley, offer you stunning scenery and the kind of freedom that's hard to find elsewhere. But your adventure doesn't have to involve epic trips. Weekend kayaking adventures, challenging hiking trails accessible via national parks' graded trail systems, or budget road trips to places you've never been to can be as life-changing as distant destinations.

The key is approaching local exploration with the same openness you'd bring to international travel. Research your destination. Talk to locals. Try experiences that aren't part of your usual routine. Distance matters less than attitude: your willingness to let familiar places surprise you. As your confidence grows from nearby exploration, you might find yourself ready for longer journeys, those that slow you down, enrich your experience, and fully immerse you.

Longer Journeys and Cultural Immersion

For the first time in decades, your schedule can be your own, with no school holidays to juggle and no sports commitments. This freedom opens opportunities for unhurried travel that allows genuine immersion: renting that cottage in Provence for several weeks, learning to cook pasta in a Sicilian taverna, or following the rhythm of seasons through New Zealand's changing landscapes.

The practical beauty of extended stays often lies in their surprising economy. Spending three weeks in a Greek village, shopping at local markets, and cooking your own meals can be more cost-effective than multiple short trips, while offering infinitely richer experiences. You have time to become a familiar face at the local café, learn a few words of the language, and understand a place's daily rhythms in ways that rushed tourism never allows.

But longer journeys aren't just about the destinations. They're also about how the duration affects you as the traveller. When you know you have weeks instead of days, you stop rushing. You linger over morning coffee, follow interesting conversations, and change plans because someone mentions a local festival. This unhurried pace becomes its own lesson, teaching you about presence that goes well beyond the journey itself.

Without children in tow, your travel becomes slower and more immersive. There's time for you to participate in a tea ceremony in Japan, learn calligraphy from a local master, or learn Irish dancing in an Irish pub. These experiences offer genuine connections across cultural boundaries that package tours rarely can. Cultural immersion through hands-on learning creates lasting change in you. Join a pottery workshop in a small village and you don't just learn to shape clay; you experience different relationships to time, craft, and community. Take cooking classes in Vietnam and you'll return home with new recipes and an expanded understanding of how food creates connection.

Food often provides your most accessible gateway to cultural understanding. Markets reveal local priorities and seasonal rhythms. Cooking classes become your lessons in history, geography, and values. Shared meals create cross-cultural exchange opportunities that change both you and your hosts.

You might use this freedom to explore your ancestral homelands, walk where your grandparents once lived, or learn about cultural traditions your family left behind generations ago. These heritage journeys can give deep insights into identity and belonging, filling in pieces of personal history that may have always been in the background. Of course, the freedom of extended travel and cultural immersion raises new questions: what if you want to go alone? For some women, this possibility is liberating; for others, it sparks delicate conversations with partners who may not understand the pull.

Solo Adventures

Travelling solo is the most freeing aspect of having an empty nest. You make every decision based on your interests, pace, and curiosity. Travelling alone isn't lonely but exciting, offering space for self-reflection that busy decades rarely allow.[2] The idea of travelling alone might also spark conversations at home. Your partner may wonder why independence is so vital or feel excluded. Navigating this carefully, with honesty about your desire for personal growth rather than rejection, helps turn potential conflict into a more profound understanding.

Emma, 61, booked three weeks in Kyoto, her first solo trip ever. *My husband didn't understand why I needed to go alone. I didn't fully understand either, until I got there.* She spent her mornings in temple gardens, afternoons learning calligraphy from a patient teacher, and evenings wandering narrow streets where no one knew her as *mother* or *wife*. Away from familiar roles, parts of herself that had fallen silent during busy parenting years began to wake. *I used to love being alone with my thoughts. Somewhere along the way, I'd forgotten that was even possible.*

When you travel alone, doors open, while group travel becomes less common. Without familiar companions to lean on, you're more likely to connect with locals, accept invitations to cultural events, or spend thoughtful time observing life around you. These interactions and reflections often turn into your most treasured memories.

Starting solo doesn't have to mean starting big. A weekend in a nearby city, staying in a small hotel, and following your interests without considering anyone else's preferences can be eye-opening. The confidence you gain from successful solo experiences, navigating unfamiliar systems, creating entertainment, and trusting your instincts goes well beyond just travel. Confidence built alone often improves your later trips with family or friends.

Shared Journeys

While solo travel provides independence and self-discovery, shared trips with your adult children and extended family can open up new chances for connection. The key is organising travel experiences that move beyond traditional parent-child roles towards genuine companionship, where everyone participates as adults with their own perspectives and preferences.

Successful family travel relies on careful planning, honouring everyone's schedules, interests, and financial comfort zones. Sometimes, travelling alongside each other works better than fully coordinated trips. Monica, 58, meets her daughter annually in a different Asian city where her daughter travels for work. They spend three days together exploring before her daughter's conference begins, creating a rhythm that respects her daughter's professional commitments while carving out dedicated time together. Other families succeed in organising individual adventures with arranged meetups: perhaps you explore coastal towns at your own pace. At the same time, your son hikes inland trails, then you reconvene for shared meals and stories.

This approach respects everyone's independence while creating genuine opportunities for connection. Your goal isn't to recreate family holidays from earlier decades but to build new shared experiences that reflect your current relationships. Whether camping under the stars, exploring regional food trails, or volunteering together at conservation projects, these adventures foster memories in a fresh emotional landscape.

Whether your adventures are solo, local, across Australia, or across continents, thoughtful preparation makes these dreams achievable.

Planning with Purpose

While passion can ignite your travel dreams, careful planning turns them into practical experiences. As you go through this life stage, financial considerations often become central to travel choices. After years of focusing on others' needs, dedicating resources to personal adventures may feel unfamiliar, and even a bit indulgent.

Strategic choices can open doors without risking your long-term security. Downsizing might free up capital for your once-in-a-lifetime journeys. Understanding your superannuation options, with professional advice if needed, ensures your travel dreams align with your overall financial wellbeing. Seniors Card benefits offer cumulative savings over time, including significant rail concessions across NSW and Queensland, loyalty programs, and travel rewards tailored to retirees.

Creative approaches extend your budget without cutting down on experiences. Shoulder-season travel significantly lowers costs while offering more relaxed, genuine encounters. House-sitting or home-swapping removes accommodation costs while providing a *living like a local experience*. Community group tours often blend camaraderie with discounted rates, especially appealing if you're a solo woman looking for safety and companionship.

Technology can change your travel planning from overwhelming to empowering. Simple translation, navigation, and accommodation booking apps remove barriers that once made solo travel seem daunting. Sharing your location with trusted contacts offers peace of mind, while translation apps can turn language barriers into conversation starters. The key is choosing one or two tools that suit your specific travel aims rather than trying to master every travel app available.

Your goal isn't extravagant spending, but intentional investing in experiences that remind you how capable, curious women travel well. Thoughtful financial planning provides the foundation, but practical safety considerations ensure your adventures unfold confidently.

Health, Safety, and Accessibility

Your travel planning must recognise physical realities without being restricted by them. Many destinations now offer accessibility options that enable exploration for people with different mobility levels: step-free trails, wheelchair-accessible transport, and guided tours that suit various fitness levels.

Comprehensive travel insurance becomes essential, especially for international trips where Medicare offers no coverage. Consulting your healthcare providers before travelling, particularly for longer journeys, ensures you're ready for routine needs and unforeseen circumstances.

Safety considerations are vital, but they shouldn't turn into barriers. Basic precautions like sharing itineraries with trusted contacts, choosing well-reviewed accommodation, and trusting your instincts establish a secure foundation for independent adventures. The confidence you build from successful travel often proves more valuable than the specific destinations you visit.

Practical Strategies

Your dreams become reality when grounded in practical steps. Here are strategies you might find helpful:

Building Your Solo Travel Confidence: Start with day trips or overnight stays within driving distance, gradually expanding your comfort zone. Book accommodation with a 24-hour reception for peace of mind, especially on your first solo adventures. Keep digital copies of important documents in cloud storage and learn basic phrases for the countries you plan to visit. Most importantly, trust your instincts. If something feels wrong to you, change plans without hesitation.

Smart Budget Planning: Travel during shoulder seasons when costs drop significantly and crowds ease. Use accommodation comparison sites but ensure you book directly with individual properties for better service and possible upgrades. Consider house-sitting through trusted platforms like TrustedHousesitters to eliminate accommodation costs while gaining authentic local experiences. Pack light to avoid baggage fees and enhance your mobility. Research free activities, such as walking tours, regional markets, public galleries, and parks, which offer rich experiences without admission costs.

The Deeper Journey

Ultimately, your travels during the empty nest phase turn potential loneliness into active exploration. Each departure and return helps you discover who you're becoming as primary caregiving duties end and new adventures begin. Your goal isn't just collecting destinations but opening up to experience and growth. Whether wandering cobblestone streets in remote villages or finding hidden gems nearby, each trip offers chances for personal growth and renewed curiosity about the world's possibilities.

Travel becomes your practice of attention to new landscapes, different ways of living, and parts of yourself that emerge when routine constraints fall away.

As your travels end, whether they've taken you across continents, along winding coastal roads, or just to the next town, you might embark on a new journey: becoming a grandparent. Much like travel, this next chapter is about connection, curiosity, and seeing the world through fresh eyes, but this time the lens is shaped by the small hands you hold and the stories you pass on. We'll explore how becoming a grandparent can broaden your identity, strengthen family bonds, and offer opportunities for joy, growth, and legacy.

Reflections and Practices

Individual Reflection Prompts

- When was the last time you briefly travelled and felt most alive? What about that experience delighted you?
- Which fears hold you back from travel right now: financial, physical, emotional, or practical? Write about where each comes from and whether it serves you.
- Imagine yourself setting out on a solo journey. What excites you most? What worries you most?

Creative Journalling Exercises

The Wander List

Write a list of 10 places you'd love to visit near or far. Now divide them into three categories: local, regional, and international. Choose one from each list and note one step you could take this month toward it.

Guided Writing Exercises

The Micro-Adventure Plan

Design a one-day or weekend journey within two hours of your home. Write out where you'd go, what you'd do, and how you'd travel. Treat it with the same respect as an overseas trip.

Reflective Questions for Deeper Exploration

- How has your definition of adventure shifted since your children left home?
- What role does travel play in how you express freedom and identity now?
- How might travel help you reconnect with parts of

yourself that feel dormant?

- Which cultural or ancestral journeys call to you, and what meaning might they hold?

Key Takeaway

Travel in the empty nest years is less about distance and more about possibility; every journey, near or far, becomes a way to rediscover freedom, curiosity, and the woman you are still becoming.

Chapter 17

Grandparenting

*H*er *heart warmed when he called her 'Nanny' for the first time. She became someone new, not a replacement for who she'd been, but an expansion of it. The woman who had once measured her days by school bus times, term breaks and sports training schedules now found herself counting in different rhythms: first words, wobbly steps, bedtime stories that stretched deliciously long because there was nowhere else she needed to be. After years of wondering what would fill the quiet house, the answer arrived wrapped in small arms and endless questions.*

As time passed, more grandchildren appeared. She would hold those babies in her arms long after they were asleep and should have been in their cots. She was unable to describe the love she felt. She felt she was the luckiest woman in the world.

Even in that pure love, she uncovered complexities she hadn't expected: balancing presence and boundaries, joy and exhaustion, privilege and pressure. This chapter examines those tensions: the remarkable gifts of grandparenting alongside its real challenges.

The Magic of Being Chosen

One of grandparenting's most meaningful gifts is the freedom it provides to focus on being present rather than chasing perfection. As someone who once worried about balanced meals, you can now enjoy the simple pleasure of licking batter from the spoon. If you are a grandfather who was once too tired after work to build blanket forts, you can now create entire pillow kingdoms with the patience of someone who finally has the time.

Lynne reflects on how this change has affected her. She no longer feels she needs to be perfect with her grandchildren; just being there is enough. They plant seeds in her garden together without worrying about perfect rows, and when they bake biscuits, it's okay if the kitchen gets covered in flour. She's not trying to teach lessons or impart life skills. She's simply loving them and discovering what love looks like in this new season.

This freedom to enjoy childhood's magic often awakens forgotten parts of yourself. David, aged sixty-nine, experienced this when his five-year-old grandson asked him to draw a dinosaur. After decades without touching a crayon, he found himself lying on the floor sketching purple T-Rexes with rainbow spots. His grandson never minded that the dinosaur looked more like a lumpy dog; he just wanted to create something together.

Becoming a grandmother is unlike any other life change you'll go through. It happens without direct involvement, job application, or deliberate choice; news from your grown-up child shifts everything. You don't choose it; it chooses you. Whether it's a long-held dream realised or a surprise, grandmotherhood remains one of life's greatest privileges: your chance to love unconditionally without bearing the primary responsibility.

The privilege is in being loved just for existing in their world. Your grandchildren don't judge your performance or choices; they enjoy your company. This unconditional acceptance fosters a special relationship that you'll probably call pure joy. When grandchildren live nearby, your presence can be simple; when they are far away, it requires a different kind of creativity from you.

When Distance Separates Hearts

Distance presents a notably modern challenge for many Australian grandparents. Research indicates that over one-third live interstate or overseas from their grandchildren, which causes genuine heartache.[1] Missing first steps, school concerts, and bedtime cuddles creates a specific grief that other grandparents might not comprehend.

Patricia moved from Sydney to Perth for her husband's job and keeps in touch with her grandchildren in Melbourne. She sends little gifts with seeds from her garden so they can grow something with Nan from afar. They schedule weekly video calls while working on the same jigsaw puzzles and chatting. She describes it as not the same as being there, but it's a genuine connection.

Distance brings genuine grief, like missing first steps, school concerts, and bedtime cuddles. Yet some grandparents find that, even though it's painful, geographic separation offers different freedoms: the chance to travel without guilt, follow uninterrupted hobbies, and keep relationships with partners without constant demands. It's not a replacement for being there, just a different reality with its own shape.

Maintaining meaningful relationships requires creativity and intention when you're separated by distance. Consistency becomes essential. You need regular contact that your grandchildren can anticipate and rely on. Creative shared activities work across distances: reading the same book simultaneously, working on matching puzzles during video calls, or sending supplies for craft projects you complete together from different cities.

Your advantage often lies in the distance that demands intentionality. Every interaction becomes deliberate rather than casual, usually forging strong bonds. Long-distance grandchildren frequently report feeling specially chosen by grandparents who make an apparent effort to stay connected despite obstacles. Geography is one challenge you face; the economics of modern family life is another.

Modern Pressures and Practical Management

Today's economic reality has fundamentally shifted grandparenting expectations. Housing costs, job instability, and childcare expenses have created a generation of parents who rely heavily on grandparental support for occasional babysitting and essential family stability.[2]

With quality childcare costing well over a hundred dollars a day, many families would struggle financially without grandparental support. Emma, from Adelaide, cared for four grandchildren across two families while her adult children worked full-time. Her daughter, a teacher, and her son-in-law, who worked in construction, faced rising mortgage and childcare costs. They would have fallen behind financially without Emma's help three days a week. She essentially ran a free childcare service, yet these were her grandchildren. The arrangement didn't feel optional.

Emma maintained this schedule for two years, believing that saying no would mean she didn't love them enough. Then the chest pains started. A trip to the emergency department and several difficult conversations with her doctor forced her to confront what she'd been avoiding: the arrangement wasn't sustainable.

When Emma tried to pull back, her son warned they'd have to sell the house. That statement haunted her sleepless nights. But her doctor stayed firm about the health risks. The family sat down for tough conversations about what was realistic, not just what felt necessary.

Eventually, they found a new balance. Emma cut back her care to one day a week instead of three. Her son adjusted his work hours, and her daughter's family arranged for part-time childcare they could afford. The budget stayed tight, but everyone was managing. Emma learnt that boundaries didn't lessen her love. Instead, they protected her ability to be present and healthy for her grandchildren in the long run.

This creates complex dynamics for many grandparents. You feel needed but sometimes taken for granted. You're grateful for the closeness but exhausted by the responsibility. You may provide significant daily care, financial support, and practical assistance, yet have little say in major decisions affecting the grandchildren you help raise. Society celebrates parents but rarely recognises the grandparents whose support makes modern family life possible.

The truth is this: while many grandparents offer vital support that helps working families, such involvement should be a choice, not an expectation. The cultural and economic forces that make grandparental help necessary can blur your right to set personal boundaries and rest. Protecting your health and wellbeing isn't selfish. Sometimes it means disappointing others temporarily, but it's the only way to stay sustainable for those you care about.

The Right to Choose

Not all grandparents want or can take on regular caregiving tasks. That's not only okay, it's healthy. After decades of raising children and making daily decisions for others, the later years should focus on rest, independence, and personal pursuits. Boundaries aren't signs of detachment; they are expressions of self-care. Love given freely, whether through occasional visits or weekly care, remains meaningful regardless of how often.

Grandparenting, at its best, is a voluntary extension of love rather than a duty. Support that is freely given, whether through occasional babysitting, shared meals, or emotional encouragement, remains valuable regardless of how often or how long it is provided. The amount of care should never be judged by the hours involved but by the intention and presence behind them.

Older generations should not feel guilt or social pressure for protecting their health, time, or independence. Boundaries are not signs of detachment; they are expressions of sustainability. Choosing not to take on intensive childcare or household duties does not lessen love; it maintains the ability to give it meaningfully. However, for many families, even clear boundaries cannot prevent situations that require more involvement.

When Care Becomes Commitment

These pressures might escalate beyond regular support into much more intensive involvement due to family crises, economic hardship, or circumstances that place grandchildren in your primary care. This can mean navigating legal guardianship, managing health and education decisions, or providing full-time care during family difficulties. The administrative complexities often frustrate families, making early access to professional support services crucial.[4]

Setting clear boundaries early prevents later exhaustion and resentment. Agreeing on your availability and limits with adult children before problems develop protects everyone involved. Saying, *I can help on Mondays, but not every day*, creates sustainable expectations rather than endless demands.

Protecting your own well-being becomes essential when you're providing frequent childcare. Your health sustains the whole family, making recovery time and self-care practical necessities rather than luxuries. If you become a primary carer, exploring kinship care services, grandparent support groups, and financial or legal advice early prevents your family from reaching a crisis point.

Simple traditions often create the most lasting memories to treasure. Friday pancake mornings, bedtime story calls, or walks in the garden become cherished rituals that your grandchildren carry into adulthood. Sharing recipes, songs, or stories from your heritage builds continuity across generations through everyday acts rather than formal lessons.

Maintaining relationships over a distance involves tools like shared calendars, which help you stay informed about school events, and voice messages, allowing children to hear your voice throughout the week. The key is consistency. Regular contact with your grandchildren can foster a sense of security, even when geography separates you. Despite routines, the tender question remains: Is advice useful, and is presence enough at times?

Full-time grandparent caregiving, whether due to family crisis, addiction, death, or other circumstances, requires support beyond what this chapter can cover. Organisations like Grandparents Raising Grandchildren provide specialised resources, legal guidance, and peer support for those navigating this challenging role.

Wisdom and Boundaries

No part of modern grandparenting is more challenging than knowing when and how to offer parenting advice. You see your adult children make choices you disagree with, repeat mistakes you could help them avoid, or face issues you've already managed. Giving guidance can risk straining relationships or being seen as meddling. This appears in everyday moments, like a toddler's meltdown tempting you to step in, screen time extending longer than you'd prefer, or discipline seeming inconsistent. What you perceive as wisdom might be taken as judgment, leaving everyone frustrated.

Sophie found that professional guidance helped her navigate this tension. Her daughter felt like a failure for needing so much support, while Sophie felt frustrated watching her struggle with problems she'd already dealt with. Through counselling, they learned to have honest conversations about when advice was welcome and when emotional support was needed. Sophie now asks whether her daughter wants suggestions or simply needs someone to listen before jumping into solutions. This simple question transformed their relationship, allowing space for both guidance and independence.

Learning to offer support while respecting boundaries becomes a continual balancing act that calls for humility and patience.[5] For some, love must travel entirely different pathways.

When Grandchildren Remain Out of Reach

Your lack of grandchildren doesn't reduce your worth or your ability to influence future generations. You might find meaningful ways to share wisdom and love with young people through mentoring, volunteering, or forming chosen family bonds. Ruth never became a grandmother but found great satisfaction as a neighbour's honorary grandmother: *I taught the little girl next door to bake bread, just like my grandmother taught me. She asked me to make the bread for her wedding reception when she got married last year. The absence of blood relation didn't diminish the love we shared.*

School volunteer programs, youth mentoring organisations, and community groups offer opportunities to build intergenerational bonds that can be as meaningful as biological grandparenting.

Estrangement from grandchildren, whether due to family conflict, divorce, or parental decisions, carries a particular grief. Unlike death, the loss is ambiguous: they're alive but unreachable. Support groups like Grandparents Australia Inc. provide a specialised understanding. Some grandparents find solace in therapy, while others advocate for grandparents' rights. The pain doesn't disappear but becomes bearable when witnessed by others who understand.

Finding Balance

When you first become a grandparent and feel your heart swell, you understand what millions know: this role offers life's sweetest joys and its most intricate challenges. Success comes from embracing the magic of being chosen by little people who believe you're magical and accepting the reality of exhaustion, boundaries, and sometimes complex negotiations. For many, this unexpected chapter answers the question that haunted the empty nest years: What comes after primary parenting ends? It's love in a completely new form.

The connections you build through grandparenting inspire you to consider the legacy you want to leave for future generations. In the next chapter, the question of what you leave behind becomes amplified with each new generation. Legacy is about inheritance, but its greatest treasure is influence, memory, and meaning.

Reflections and Practices

Creative Journalling Exercises

The Generational Tree

Sketch a simple family tree. Instead of focusing only on names and dates, note down values, sayings, or traditions you'd like to see passed along. Highlight those you want to carry forward and those you're ready to release.

The Boundary Conversation
Draft the words you might use to express boundaries lovingly to your adult child (e.g., time limits, financial support). Practising the language on paper makes real-life conversations easier.

Ongoing Check-Ins
- Did I make one meaningful moment of connection this week with my grandchild, family, or a younger person in my community?
- Am I balancing joy in grandparenting with care for my own needs?
- What small memory or ritual did I help create that could last beyond me?

Partner/Group Discussion Prompts
- How do we want to shape our shared role as grandparents? What do we each bring?
- How can we support our adult children while respecting their independence?
- What intergenerational traditions or new rituals could we build together?

Key Takeaway
Grandparenting is more about presence than perfection. Whether through bedtime stories, long-distance video calls, or chosen family connections, it allows love across generations while balancing joy with boundaries.

Chapter 18

Legacy: What Will You Leave Behind?

S he stood in the record office in Belfast, tracing names with her finger along fading registers. Each name was a thread in a tapestry that stretched across oceans. Every visit to Ireland deepened the connection; whenever someone greeted her with, "How long are you home for?" She felt the truth of belonging to two places at once. Legacy, she observed, wasn't only what you left behind; it was what you carried, shared, and nurtured.

She turned to her family's Irish roots to anchor her newfound freedom. This search for legacy filled the emotional space left by their absence, blending grief with purpose. Tracing her family history became a devoted pursuit. She researched names, gathered stories, and built bridges between relatives in Australia and Ireland through ancestry and shared heritage. She wasn't content to keep it to herself. She joined a cultural association, creating space for others' stories. She told the stories of Irish Australians who had shaped society and culture, both historically and today.

With your roots acknowledged and claimed, the next question hits closer to home: What do your daily relationships offer the next generation? A Walter Butler Palmer poem might express something you've felt but couldn't quite name. It could be the longing to be remembered, to matter across time. You might find yourself returning to the last stanza.

Dear Ancestor, the place you filled
One hundred years ago
Spreads out among the ones you left
Who would have loved you so
I wonder how you lived and loved
I wonder if you knew.
That someday I would find this spot.
And come to visit you.

Sitting with your records and stories, you might wonder what your children and their children will inherit from you. Hopefully, it's not just the names and dates of past generations, but a sense of belonging, a love of learning, and the understanding that legacy is something you value and live truly every day.

The Heart of Family Legacy

Your legacy starts in the heart of your home. Long before your children left, you shaped their future through the stories you shared, the boundaries you set, the compassion you showed, and how you mended your mistakes. When your nest empties, you often look back on those formative years with clearer eyes. At its core, your legacy is about relationships. It's built on how you've loved, supported others, and consistently shown up. Maya Angelou captured this perfectly: People will forget what you said and what you did, but they will never forget how you made them feel.[1]

A woman who mentored teenagers realised her legacy

years later when one of them got in touch. The young woman told her she'd made her feel safe for the first time and showed her that adults could be trusted. That is legacy in its most generous form.

Emotional legacy resides in small, repeated gestures that provide security and love. It's about being the person they turn to when something remarkable happens and when everything falls apart. Reflecting on it, you might ask yourself: Did you embody the values you hope to pass on? Did your children inherit your empathy, resilience, humour, or creativity? Maybe they absorbed something less obvious: your adaptability, your ability to apologise, or the simple act of starting over with grace.

One woman realised her proudest legacy wasn't a family heirloom or property. It was watching her daughter stop to comfort a stranger on the street. In that moment, she knew her daughter had inherited her values, not just her name.

Stories as Living Gifts

Your legacy today is recorded in diaries or passed down by word of mouth. Your digital, environmental, and social choices also shape it. Stories connect generations by sharing facts and feelings, reminding us of who we are, where we've come from, and what we value. You now have the chance to reflect on and document your life stories, not necessarily for publication, but for safekeeping.

In some Australian communities, storytelling through yarning is a sacred, relational act that conveys knowledge, resilience, and a profound sense of belonging. Similarly, your memoirs, handwritten letters, photo albums, and family anecdotes become everyday heirlooms.

For one farm woman, songs became her most treasured offering. The same lullabies her mother had sung to her in a gentle Irish lilt, she had sung to her own daughters through feverish nights and restless bedtimes, and now she sang them to her grandchildren. These were melodies, memories made audible; grief transformed into comfort, and history carried in the cadence of a voice. She began writing them down, carefully noting the words her mother had taught her; some in Irish, some in English, worn smooth by generations of singing. She recorded herself, her voice cracking slightly on the high notes, laughing at her imperfections, knowing that someday those imperfections would be what made the recordings precious.

She compiled them into a book for her family, including handwritten lyrics, annotations about the origins of each song, stories about her grandmother, and how her mother would hum them while kneading bread, as well as how she had rocked her daughters to sleep with the same verses. It wasn't a perfect collection; some verses had been lost to time, and she could only partly remember some words and melodies. It was a legacy of continuity, proof that love could travel across centuries in four-minute songs, and that her grandchildren would sing the exact words their great-great-grandmother had sung in a farmhouse in County Tyrone.

When she showed the collection to her daughters, one of them began crying. The youngest said she'd been trying to remember the words to a particular song for years, the one about the blackboard, and thought it was lost forever. Now it was saved. Now it would go on.

Another woman created a digital storytelling project for

her goddaughter while she was undergoing cancer treatment. She said *I didn't know if I'd be here to see her grow up. But I wanted her to understand what I stood for.* Another used virtual reality tools to craft a tour of her childhood Sydney suburb, blending her past with her grandchildren's future.

Whether you type, record on your phone, or write in a journal, these stories are acts of generosity from you. Start small: choose one memory, a moment that shaped, challenged, or made you laugh. Record it or jot it down. Even one preserved story can become a treasured legacy. Research shows that storytelling strengthens intergenerational bonds, supports identity, and boosts resilience in young people.

You might also curate digital scrapbooks on Instagram or Facebook, turning photo grids into modern memory boxes. Others use voice-note apps or AI transcription tools to preserve spoken stories for children and grandchildren. Your legacy lives both in the cloud and at the kitchen table, and the stories you carry don't stop at your front gate; they ripple into your community.

Future-Facing Legacies

Your legacy isn't just engraved on headstones or tucked away in handwritten letters. It also exists in the digital world, where voice notes and video journals can carry your tone, laughter, and warmth long after you're gone. AI transcription helps preserve family stories as searchable memory archives. Meanwhile, carefully curated social media feeds become modern scrapbooks, galleries of moments that future generations can scroll through like pages in a photo album.

Legacy can also connect to the land beneath your feet.

Planting trees with grandchildren, regenerating farmland, or choosing sustainable living practices are everyday acts that ripple out in unseen ways. They are commitments to a future you might not see, but one you actively shape. Your garden becomes a living heirloom, offering seasonal gifts that remind your family of resilience and care. Cutting down waste or joining Landcare groups creates an environmental legacy rooted in care for the planet your descendants will inherit.

Yet your legacy extends beyond bloodlines and land. Mentoring a younger colleague, volunteering at a women's shelter, or joining local activism for climate or justice ensures that your values outlive you. As one woman reflected, *My legacy isn't my surname; it's the confidence I helped unlock in younger women.* These contributions defy time, measured not in property or possessions but in courage multiplied across lives. Julie never had children, but her legacy lived through mentoring young women at her local community centre, who called her 'Aunty' and carried her wisdom forward. Another woman helped lead a multicultural festival, while others contributed to language revitalisation programs or planted native trees in community gardens with their grandchildren, weaving environmental care into shared legacies.

Your mentorship becomes a meaningful legacy too: teaching a neighbour's daughter to sew, guiding a younger colleague at work, or sharing farming wisdom with a new generation. Where could your skills or wisdom make a difference? However you answer, these acts defy short-term thinking and ripple forward in ways you may never fully see.

Planning With Care

While your legacy is often emotional and cultural, practical planning is essential, too. For many women, especially those in rural or lower-income households, your financial legacy isn't about lump sums. It's about order, fairness, and clarity.

Practical legacy planning matters too, especially for women who want to ensure fairness and clarity after they're gone. As of 2023, only 53% of Australian adults had current, valid wills, often leading to family disputes and stress.[2]

Val, 61, finally updated her will after watching her sister's family fracture over their mother's unclear estate. Her mother had always promised to sort it out later, but later never came. Suddenly, Val and her sister weren't speaking over a house that neither of them even wanted. Val swore she would never put her own children through that pain.

Resources exist to help: Public Trustee offices provide affordable will-writing, community legal centres offer free advice for low-income people, and superannuation funds assist with beneficiary nominations. Small steps, like one conversation or one signed document, can prevent future pain for the people you love most.[3]

You might decide to leave charitable gifts, like a small bequest to a cause you've long supported. You could establish educational funds or contribute to community initiatives. Small steps matter to you: one conversation, one signed document, one preserved memory at a time. Your legacy isn't just what you pass on; it's also what you choose not to keep passing along.

Breaking the Chains

Your legacy isn't just about what you aim to pass on; it also includes what you decide to leave behind. Family patterns of dysfunction might seem like inherited curses, but you can break them through conscious choice. Often, your legacy work involves passing things down and intentionally stopping transmission.

Breaking generational cycles isn't about being perfect yourself. It's about taking responsibility where you can and creating new patterns. The grandmother who seeks help for her drinking problem, knowing her family history with alcohol. The mother who learns to apologise when she's wrong, breaking a cycle of authoritarian parenting. The aunt who refuses to continue family patterns of criticism and favouritism. These choices open up new possibilities.

Sometimes, your legacy is also playful. There's the family joke that will outlive you, the playlist you made for your grandchildren, or the recipe no one else can quite get right. These small gifts carry warmth forward just as surely as your bigger choices.

Consider Leonie, whose mother's anxiety had shaped three generations of women in her family. When her own daughter began showing signs of inherited worry patterns, Leonie sought therapy not just for herself but to understand how anxiety had been unconsciously learned and passed down. She learned to recognise her feelings, manage her responses, and talk openly about mental health, creating a new family language around emotional well-being.

When you pay for your daughter's therapy despite financial struggles, when you choose not to repeat harmful words that damaged your own childhood, and when you treat all grandchildren equally, refusing to show favouritism, these are acts of deliberate interruption that may never be recognised, but they change everything. Your conscious change, repeated over time, becomes a way of life.

Living Practice, Not Final Destination

Your legacy isn't what you leave behind; it's how you live now. Through kindness given, stories shared, courage passed on, how you listen, the boundaries you set, and the compassion you show in everyday moments.

Your legacy isn't about seeking immortality or controlling how you'll be remembered. It's about living intentionally, loving consistently, and contributing to the human story in ways that reflect your core values. The question isn't whether you'll leave a legacy, because you already do, simply by living and touching the lives of others. The real question is whether that legacy truly reflects who you are and what you most want to pass on.

The good news is that it's never too late to begin. The most powerful part of your legacy is the life you're still shaping. Your nest may be empty, but the life you've lived continues to resonate in the hearts of others. Your children, neighbours, colleagues, and communities carry traces of your presence, often in ways you might not even notice. Your legacy isn't a monument but a living current, still alive and evolving. And perhaps the best gift of the empty nest is this reminder: it's never too late to influence that current, never too late to live the story you most want to leave behind.

Because in the end, your legacy is not the echo of absence,

but the presence you leave in others. Your nest may be empty, but your life is still whole, and its story is far from finished.

Reflections and Practices

Individual Reflection Prompts

- What do you hope your children or community will remember most about you?
- Which values have you lived that you'd like others to carry forward?
- Think about one person who influenced you profoundly. How did their "legacy" show up in your life?

Guided Writing Exercises

Breaking Chains: List one family pattern you want to end consciously. Then, write the alternative behaviour or practice you choose instead.

Living Legacy: Describe three small daily actions that quietly build your legacy, e.g., listening fully, planting a garden, volunteering, cooking with love.

Your Legacy Letter

Write a letter to a future grandchild, real or imagined. Share a hope, a lesson, or a story you want them to know. What do you want them to understand about who you were, what you valued, and what brought you joy? Don't worry about perfect words. Think about the emotional tone you want to leave. What would you want them to feel when they read your words years from now?

Key Takeaway

Legacy lives in the everyday: in the choices you make, the values you uphold, and the relationships you cultivate, each leaving a footprint that endures long after you.

Chapter 19

Letting Go

Another harvest is just weeks away. Hopefully one of our last. It's a busy time of year, a time of reward for the farmers who gamble with the seasons through strength, determination, and reliability. Yet within these walls, I am steady.

This farmhouse has become my sanctuary, bright, airy, and softened by years of living. It holds the laughter, worry, the growing-up years, and now, I've learned to love this solitude. I walk through each room with peace, knowing I have shaped it, and it has shaped me.

Once filled with my daughters' laughter and the hum of motorbikes, the paddocks rest in stillness. Their boots no longer line the back door, and their music has dissolved into time. They've built their own worlds beyond these fields, close enough to reach yet far enough to remind me that life keeps moving on, and so do I.

I now watch their world with love and gentle pride. I enjoy babysitting and love their children. Though I once felt the ache of their absence deeply, I've moved past that phase. The house isn't quite so empty anymore, and it's always open. This is a home where I've started again. The empty nest has become an opportunity to reframe, restructure, and reimagine the rest of *my years.*

Sadness still visits, as all meaningful things do. These days, it lingers briefly before drifting on. I understand it better now. Time has moved forward, and so have I.

Whatever comes next, I'm not afraid. This place, and this life, have prepared me for change.

Reflections on the Journey

This book began with a realisation that I was not the only mother to see her children leave. This question has remained with me. I could find no guide for this moment because the silence surrounding the experience of an empty nest pressed more heavily than dust ever did.

We started with preparations and reflected on tender goodbyes. We sat with loneliness and then explored our identity, questioning what was lost and what might be found. We celebrated freedom, discussed reimagining the home, and turned to relationships with partners, adult children, friends, and community. We examined returning to work, rediscovering purpose, and grandparenting as a form of love. We concluded with legacy: the stories we share or withhold, the wisdom we pass on, and the lives we influence.

These themes have shaped the last twenty years of my life. They came into focus gradually, like dawn over frosted paddocks. Each reader has their own version of this journey, but I hope you've found echoes of your experience within these pages.

To the woman navigating this difficult time, I see you. To the one celebrating it, I applaud you. I wrote this for every woman who has stood in the hallway, suitcase in hand, bedroom door ajar. I began with silence and questions, and I end with something else: not answers, perhaps, but peace.

A Life Reimagined

The nest might be still, but your story is far from finished. Throughout rural and coastal towns, leafy suburbs, and busy cities, women are waking up to a new kind of morning. The children have grown, the rhythm has shifted, and what comes next is uncharted.

This journey isn't simple or neat. You might still feel waves of sadness or longing; those feelings don't vanish just because a book is finished or time has passed. Perhaps you've found comfort in knowing you're not alone. Your experience is shared in the profoundly human way of people whose lives have been upended by love, responsibility, and the courage to let go.

Progress isn't always linear. Some days might feel like a step back into sadness or doubt, especially when routines change again or milestones go unnoticed. But those moments don't wipe out how far you've already come. Even in stillness, you're still progressing. You are growing, even in stillness.

One truth remains clear: the empty nest is simply a fresh start in the last half-century of our lives. You can be many things now: a grandparent, a volunteer, a traveller, a lover, a learner, a maker, a friend. You can explore new paths, change your mind, or take a breath. You don't need to prove anything or do anything. You get to be.

Small Changes, Real Shifts

Transformation isn't abrupt. Often, it's a slow process. You don't need to reinvent yourself completely to feel rejuvenated. Small acts matter. Think of a new hobby, a long walk, or re-connecting with a forgotten friend. Over time, these things accumulate into a new sense of self that honours the past but isn't limited by it.

You might not notice the changes as they happen, but they do. Staying close to home, deepening your routines, or finding new joy in familiar places is a form of renewal. You don't need to change your world to be changed by it.

What Endures

As you look ahead, recognise what's already strong: the child who calls, the neighbour you helped, the hours you dedicated to your community, the friendships that lasted, and the kindness you showed when no one was watching. These aren't trivial things. They're the foundation of the life you've built, supporting whatever comes next. What you do now leaves a mark, not just in your life but also in what others see as possible. This next chapter will resonate with the lives of your children, grandchildren, and younger women observing from the edges.

A Gentle Prompt for the Road Ahead

Pause here, just for a moment. Not to plan, fix, or look too far ahead, but to recognise where you are now: a woman who has raised others and is returning to herself. A woman with more time, space, and control over her destiny, ready to ask, *What do I want from here?*

You don't need a five-year plan or a grand new project. A phone call, a walk, or a rest will do. The page ahead is blank. You're not late. You are exactly where you need to be.

The invitation remains curious. Take up space, rest, reconnect, stay visible, and write the next bit gently, boldly, or however you choose.

A Closing Reflection

For every mother who has let go and still loves fiercely, this is for you.

And still, the dust gathers. But now, it settles around a life that has been reimagined.

End Notes

Chapter 1

[1] Australian Seniors. (2024). Empty nesters report 2024: Boomerang kids are returning to the nest, but empty nesters would prefer their space.

[2] Boss, P. (2006). *Loss, trauma, and resilience: Therapeutic work with ambiguous loss.* W.W. Norton.

[3] Novak, L. (2018, September 25). *Research shows that parents still worry about grown children.* DoYouRemember. https://doyouremember.com/85108/parents-still-worry-about-grown-children

[4] Trautmann, S. *Empty nest syndrome: Parents are happiest when their kids grow up.* Fatherly. https://www.fatherly.com/health/empty-nest-syndrome-parents-happiest-when-kids-grow-up

[5] Psychiatric Association of Greece. (2019). Empty-nest-related psychosocial stress: Conceptual issues, future directions in economic crisis. Psychiatriki, 30(4), 329–338. https://www.psychiatriki-journal.gr/documents/psychiatry/30.4-EN-2019-329.pdf

[6] Goleman, D. (1995). *Emotional intelligence: Why it can matter more than IQ.* Bantam Books.

Chapter 2

[1] Australian Bureau of Statistics. (2019). *Family transitions and household formation.*

[2] Beyond Blue. (2021). The mental health of Australians in midlife: Stress, menopause, and life transitions.

[3] McCubbin, H. I., & Patterson, J. M. (1983). The family stress process: The Double ABCX model of adjustment and adaptation. In H. McCubbin et al. (Eds.), *Social stress and the family* (pp. 7–37). Routledge.

[4] Kiecolt-Glaser, J. K., & Glaser, R. (2002). Depression and immune function: Central pathways to morbidity and mortality. *Journal of Psychosomatic Research, 53*(4), 873–876. https://doi.org/10.1016/S0022-3999(02)00309-4

[5] Mitchell, B. A., & Lovegreen, L. D. (2009). The empty nest syndrome in midlife families: A multi-generational perspective. *Journal of Family Issues*, 30(12), 1651–1670. https://doi.org/10.1177/0192513X09336667

[6] Rubin, R. (2017). When parents let go: The empty nest and identity shifts in mothers. *Journal of Women & Aging*, 29(3), 201–219. https://doi.org/10.1080/08952841.2016.1182114

[7] Umberson, D., Pudrovska, T., & Reczek, C. (2010). Parenthood, childlessness, and well-being: A life course perspective. *Journal of Marriage and Family*, 72(3), 612–629. https://doi.org/10.1111/j.1741-3737.2010.00721.x

Chapter 3

[1] Archer, M. (2019). Cultural scripts and family transitions: A cross-cultural analysis. *Journal of Family Studies*, 25(3), 289–305.

[2] Fiese, B. H., & Sameroff, A. J. (1999). Cultural scripts: How culture shapes family stories. *Family Process, 38*(4), 399–408.

[3] Bedford, O., & Yeh, K.-H. (2019). The history and the future of the psychology of filial piety: Chinese norms to contextualised personality construct. *Frontiers in Psychology, 10*, 100. https://doi.org/10.3389/fpsyg.2019.00100

[4] Joseph, S. (1999). Intimate selving in Arab families: Gender, self, and identity. Syracuse University Press.

[5] Pike, I. L., & Hilton, C. (2019). Cultural stress, menopause, and embodiment: Global perspectives on the female midlife transition. *Social Science & Medicine*, 222, 74–82. https://doi.org/10.1016/j.socscimed.2018.12.015

[6] Australian Housing and Urban Research Institute (AHURI). (2022). *Young adults, housing affordability and intergenerational living.* AHURI Final Report No. 383. https://www.ahuri.edu.au/research/final-reports/383

[5] Newman, K. S. (2012). The accordion family: Boomerang kids, anxious parents, and the private toll of global competition. Beacon Press

[6] Boss, P. (1999). Ambiguous loss: Learning to live with unresolved grief. Harvard University Press.

[7] Berndt, R. M., & Berndt, C. H. (1999). *The world of the first Australians: Aboriginal traditional life, past and present* (5th ed.). Aboriginal Studies Press.

[8] Markus, A., & Kirpitchenko, L. (2021). Australia's multicultural families: Patterns of interdependence and independence. *Journal of Intercultural Studies*, 42(5), 601–618. https://doi.org/10.1080/07256868.2021.1977167

Chapter 4

[1] Relationships Australia. (2023). *Empty nesters: Navigating life transitions.* https://www.relationships.org.au/empty-nesters/

Chapter 5

[1] SBS News. (2023, August 31). *The young Australian adults who aren't moving out of their parents' home.* SBS. https://www.sbs.com.au/news/article/the-young-australian-

adults-who-arent-moving-out-of-their-parents-home/
oc43f4ofh

[2] Institute for Social & Economic Research. (2023, February 27). *Rocketing number of adults moving back in with their parents nears five million.* University of Essex. https://www.iser.essex. ac.uk/research/news/2023/02/27/rocketing-number-of-adults-moving-back-in-with-their-parents-nears-five-million%EF%B-F%BC?utm_source=chatgpt.com

[3] Organisation for Economic Co-operation and Development. (2024). OECD *family database*: SF1.3 – *Living arrangements of young adults.* OECD. https://www.oecd.org/en/data/datasets/ oecd-family-database.html

[4] Adelaide Now. (2024, July 8). *Demand for granny flats proof of desire for housing options.* News Corp Australia. https://www. adelaidenow.com.au/real-estate/south-australia/adelaide/de-mand-for-granny-flats-proof-of-desire-for-housing-options/ news-story/796fa3cd3f334ad514af2f210dc28055

[5] Organisation for Economic Co-operation and Devel-opment. (2025). OECD *Employment Outlook 2025: De-mographic change, economic growth and intergenerational inequalities.* OECD Publishing. https://www.oecd.org/en/ publications/oecd-employment-outlook-2025_194a94

Chapter 6

[1] Jean Hailes for Women's Health. (2022). *National Women's Health Survey.* Jean Hailes for Women's Health. https://www.jean-hailes.org.au/contents/documents/Research/National-Wom-ens-Health-Survey-2022.pdf

[2] Women's Agenda. (2024). *The midlife report: Women, menopause, and mood.* Women's Agenda. https://womensagenda.com.au

[3] Australian Institute of Health and Welfare. (2023). *Health care*

access in rural and remote Australia. AIHW. https://www.aihw.gov.au/reports/rural-remote-australians/health-care-access

⁴ Wolf, N. (2002). The beauty myth: How images of beauty are used against women. Harper Perennial.

⁵ Australian Seniors. (2025). *The Sandwich Generation Report*. Australian Seniors Research Series. https://www.seniors.com.au

⁶ Carers Australia. (2023). *Caring and burnout: The state of carers in Australia*. Carers Australia. https://www.carersaustralia.com.au

⁷ Women's Agenda. (2024). *Invisibility in midlife: Survey of Australian women aged 45–65*. Women's Agenda. https://womensagenda.com.au

⁸ Lopez, S. H., & Calasanti, T. (2022). Ageing and gender in media: The invisibility of older women. *Journal of Women & Aging, 34*(4), 421–437. https://doi.org/10.1080/08952841.2021.1970234

⁹ Coupland, J., & Williams, A. (2021). Pro-ageing campaigns and the politics of visibility. *Journal of Consumer Culture, 21*(3), 456–475. https://doi.org/10.1177/14695405209477

¹⁰ ltahawy, M. (2019). The seven necessary sins for women and girls. Beacon Press.

Chapter 7

¹ Ending Loneliness Together. (2023, August 7). *One in three Australians feel lonely despite digital connections*. ABC News. https://www.abc.net.au/news/2023-08-07/ending-loneliness-together-finds-33-per-cent-australians-lonely/102678790

² Australian Seniors. (2024). *Empty Nesters Report 2024*. Australian Seniors Series. https://www.seniors.com.au/documents/seniors-empty-nesters-report-2024-whitepaper-final.pdf

³ Australian Institute of Health and Welfare. (2022). *Loneliness and social isolation in Australia*. AIHW. https://www.aihw.

gov.au/reports/mental-health/mental-health-services-in-aus-tralia/report-contents/mental-health-impact-of-covid-19/loneliness-and-social-isolation

[4] ABC. (2019, March 25). *Ladies, we need to talk: Loneliness* [Audio podcast episode]. In Y. Lee (Host), *ABC Radio*. Australian Broadcasting Corporation. https://www.abc.net.au/radio/programs/ladies-we-need-to-talk/

[5] Ong, A. D., Uchino, B. N., & Wethington, E. (2016). Loneliness and health in older adults: A mini-review and synthesis. *Journal of Positive Psychology*, 11(3), 257–265. https://doi.org/10.1080/17439760.2015.1025424

Chapter 8

[1] Relationships Australia. (2024). *Empty nesters.* https://www.relationships.org.au/empty-nesters/

[2] Australian Seniors. (2024). *Empty nesters report.* https://www.seniors.com.au/news-insights/australian-seniors-series-empty-nesters-report-2024

[3] Hartanto, A., Jiang, Y., & Lee, S. (2024). Cultural contexts differentially shape parents' loneliness and well-being during the empty-nest period. *Communications Psychology*, 2(1), 1–12. https://doi.org/10.1038/s44271-024-00156-8

[4] ABC News. (2024, May 4). *Parents suffering from empty nest syndrome reflect on their ways of coping.* Retrieved August 2025, from https://www.abc.net.au/news/2024-05-04/coping-with-empty-nest-syndrome/103708176

[5] The Guardian. (2024, February 10). *'It was time to start afresh': Readers on love in an empty nest.* Retrieved August 2025, from https://www.theguardian.com/lifeandstyle/2024/feb/10/relationship-changes-marriage-kids-move-out-empty-nest

[6] Dennerstein, L., Dudley, E., & Guthrie, J. (2002). Empty nest or revolving door? A prospective study of women's quality of life in midlife during the phase of children leaving and re-entering the home. *Psychological Medicine*, 32(3), 545–550. https://doi.org/10.1017/S0033291702005439

[7] Choi, H., & Marks, N. (2008). Transition to empty nest and parents' well-being: A longitudinal study. *The Journals of Gerontology: Series B*, 63(3), S135–S143. https://doi.org/10.1093/geronb/63.3.S135

[8] Johnson, R. (1986). *She: Understanding feminine psychology.* Harper & Row.

Chapter 9
[1] Lorde, A. (1988). *A burst of light: Essays.* Firebrand Books.

[2] InStyle. (2024, March 21). Brooke Shields on the freedom of becoming an empty nester. *InStyle Magazine.* https://www.instyle.com/brooke-shields-empty-nester-freedom

[3] People. (2023, October 4). Naomi Watts says menopause can be empowering in 'Hotter Than Ever' campaign. *People Magazine.* https://people.com/naomi-watts-stripes-beauty-hotter-than-ever

[4] Cryan, J. F., O'Riordan, K. J., Cowan, C. S. M., Sandhu, K. V., Bastiaanssen, T. F. S., Boehme, M., ... & Dinan, T. G. (2019). The microbiota–gut–brain axis. *Physiological Reviews*, 99(4), 1877–2013. https://doi.org/10.1152/physrev.00018.2018

[5] McMillan, J. (2018). Get lean, stay lean: The 6-step program for a happier, healthier body, for life. Murdoch Books.

[6] Jean Hailes for Women's Health. (2023). *Food & nutrition for midlife women.* https://www.jeanhailes.org.au/health-a-z/food-nutrition

[7] Doyle, G. (2020). *Untamed.* Dial Press.

[8] Clear, J. (2018). Atomic habits: An easy & proven way to build good habits & break bad ones. Avery.

[10] BMC Public Health. (2023). Loneliness and social isolation have a mortality risk similar to cigarette smoking, alcohol consumption, physical inactivity, and obesity. *BMC Public Health.*

Chapter 10

[1] Camus, A. (1961). Resistance, Rebellion, and Death (J. O'Brien, Trans.). Knopf/Vintage. (Original essays published 1946–1957).

[2] Giurge, L. M., Whillans, A. V., & West, C. (2020). Why time poverty matters for individuals, organisations and nations. *Nature Human Behaviour*, 4, 993–1003. https://doi.org/10.1038/s41562-020-0920-z

[3] Sturm, V. E., Datta, S., Roy, A. R. K., & Killgore, W. D. S. (2023). Small moments of awe promote well-being in everyday life. *Psychological Science*, 34(2), 227–237. https://doi.org/10.1177/09567976221134779

[4] Moen, P., & Flood, S. (2022). Parenting transitions and women's identities in midlife. *Journal of Marriage and Family*, 84(3), 745–761. https://doi.org/10.1111/jomf.12849

[5] Ryan, R. M., & Deci, E. L. (2020). Intrinsic and extrinsic motivation from a self-determination theory perspective: Definitions, theory, practices, and future directions. *Contemporary Educational Psychology, 61*, 101860. https://doi.org/10.1016/j.cedpsych.2020.101860

Chapter 11

[1] Michaels, M. (2015). *The Inspired Room*. Harvest House.

[2] Kondo, M. (2014). *The Life-Changing Magic of Tidying Up*. Ten Speed Press.

[3]. Ford, L., & Ford, S. (2019). Work in Progress: Unconventional Thoughts on Designing an Extraordinary Life. HarperCollins

Chapter 12
[1] Australian Institute of Family Studies. (2022). *Divorce and separation among older Australians.* AIFS. https://aifs.gov.au

[2] Halford, W. K., & Pepping, C. A. (2023). Relationship transitions in midlife: Stress points and resilience factors. *Journal of Family Psychology,* 37(2), 145–158.

[3] Perel, E. (2017). *The State of Affairs: Rethinking infidelity.* HarperCollins.

[4] Jean Hailes for Women's Health. (2023). *Midlife health and intimacy after menopause.* https://www.jeanhailes.org.au

[5] Carers Australia. (2022). *Caring in the sandwich generation.* Carers Australia. https://www.carersaustralia.com.au

[6] Grattan Institute. (2023). The Intergenerational Report: Financial pressures on families and retirement. https://grattan.edu.au

[7] Lerner, H. (2005). *The Dance of Connection.* HarperCollins.

Chapter 13
[1] Bumble Inc. (2023). *Bumble BFF and friendship apps usage trends.* Retrieved from https://bumble.com

[2] Swinburne University & VicHealth. (2023). *Australian Loneliness Report.* Melbourne: Swinburne University.

[3] Waldinger, R., & Schulz, M. (2023). The Good Life: Lessons from the World's Longest Scientific Study of Happiness. Simon & Schuster.

[4] Buettner, D. (2023). *The Blue Zones Secrets for Living Longer.* National Geographic.

[5] Dunbar, R. (2021). Friends: Understanding the Power of Our Most Important Relationships. Little, Brown.

[6] Brown, B. (2017). *Braving the Wilderness: The Quest for True Belonging and the Courage to Stand Alone*. Random House.

[7] University of the Third Age (U3A) Network Victoria. (2023). *About U3A*. Retrieved from https://u3avictoria.com.au

[8] Australian Men's Shed Association. (2023). *Men's Sheds in Australia*. Retrieved from https://mensshed.org

[9] Empty Nest Support Network Australia. (2023). *Community forums*. [Facebook group].

[10] Heart Foundation. (2023). *Walking groups*. Heart Foundation Australia. Retrieved from https://walking.heartfoundation.org.au

[11] Parkrun Australia. (2023). *About Parkrun*. Retrieved from https://parkrun.com.au

[12] Relationships Australia. (2023). Relationships Indicators Survey 2023: Connection in Post-COVID Australia. Relationships Australia.

Chapter 14

[1] Productivity Commission (2021). *Working from Home*. https://www.pc.gov.au/research/completed/working-from-home

[2] Stone, C., & O'Shea, S. (2019). *Older Women, Lifelong Learning and Widening Participation*. National Centre for Student Equity in Higher Education. https://www.ncsehe.edu.au/older-women-lifelong-learning/

[3] Australian Human Rights Commission & Australian HR Institute. (2023). *Employing and Retaining Older Workers Report*. https://humanrights.gov.au/about/news/media-releases/ageism-keeping-older-people-out-workforce

[4] National Seniors Australia. (2021). *Age Discrimination in the Labour Market*. https://nationalseniors.com.au/research/discrimination/age-discrimination-in-the-labour-market

[5] Alston, M. (2012). *Rural Women and Leadership in Australia*.

RIRDC Publication No. 12/065. https://www.agrifutures.com.au/wp-content/uploads/publications/12-065.pdf

[6] Crawford School of Public Policy (2025). *Ageism in Job Search: A Panel Study.* Australian National University. https://crawford.anu.edu.au/ttpi/content-centre/research/ageism-job-search-panel-study

[7] ABC News. (2020). *Mature-age job seekers face workplace discrimination.* https://www.abc.net.au/news/2020-05-01/mature-age-job-seekers-workplace-discrimination-jobs-online/12187272

[8] Department of Employment and Workplace Relations. (2021). *Employment Barriers for Mature-Age Australians Research Project.* https://www.dewr.gov.au/kar/download/13806/employment-barriers-mature-age-australians-research-project/27053/employment-barriers-mature-age-australians-research-project/pdf

[9] Jobs and Skills Australia. (2024). *Mature Age Workers and the Labour Market – REOS Special Report.* https://www.jobsandskills.gov.au/news mature-age-workers-and-labour-market-reos-special-report

Chapter 15

[1] Australian Institute of Health and Welfare. (2023). *Telehealth use during COVID-19 and beyond.* https://www.aihw.gov.au/reports/primary-health-care/telehealth-use

[2] Australian Banking Association. (2023). *Bank branch closure trends in Australia.* https://www.ausbanking.org.au

[3] Services Australia. (2024). *Digital service delivery and online access.* https://www.servicesaustralia.gov.au

[4] Australian Institute of Health and Welfare. (2024). *Telehealth activity statistics.* https://www.aihw.gov.au

[5] Reserve Bank of Australia. (2023). *Trends in payments, banking, and digital adoption.* https://www.rba.gov.au

[6] MyGov. (2024). *What you can do on myGov.* https://www.my.gov.au

[7] Good Things Foundation Australia. (2024). *Be Connected program.* https://www.beconnected.esafety.gov.au

[8] NSW Government. (2023). *Tech Savvy Seniors program.* https://www.sl.nsw.gov.au/public-library-services/learning/tech-savvy-seniors

[9] NBN Co. (2024). *Regional rollout and connectivity updates.* https://www.nbnco.com.au

[10] ACCC. (2024). *Scamwatch: Annual scam statistics.* https://www.scamwatch.gov.au

[11] Australian Cyber Security Centre. (2023). *Protect yourself online: Cybersecurity tips.* https://www.cyber.gov.au

[12] ABC News. (2024). *How Australians are using AI tools in everyday life.* https://www.abc.net.au/news

[13] Change.org Australia. (2023). *About us.* https://www.change.org

Chapter 16

[1] de Botton, A. (2002). *The art of travel.* Hamish Hamilton.

[2] Wilson, E., & Harris, C. (2006). Meaningful travel: Women, independent travel and the search for self and meaning. *Tourism,* 54(2), 161–172. https://doi.org/10.1007/BF03216607

[3] Onyx, J., & Leonard, R. (2005). Australian grey nomads and "white settlers": New leisure lifestyles and retirement. *Annals of Leisure Research,* 8(1), 50–61. https://doi.org/10.1080/11745398.2005.10600941

Chapter 17

[1] ABS. (2023). *Family characteristics and transitions*. Australian Bureau of Statistics.

[2] AIHW. (2022). *Grandparent care in Australia*. Australian Institute of Health and Welfare.

[3] Australian Seniors. (2024). The Grandparent Report: Intergenerational bonds in modern Australia.

[4] Journal of Family Psychology. (2023). "Grandparenthood and emotional well-being: A longitudinal study." *Journal of Family Psychology*, 37(4), 512–526.

[5] Australian Institute of Family Studies. (2022). *Grandparenting in contemporary Australia*

Chapter 18

[1] Angelou, M. (1993). *Wouldn't take nothing for my journey now*. Random House.

[2] Australian Bureau of Statistics. (2023). *Household decisions and end-of-life planning survey*. ABS Catalogue No. 4102.0. Retrieved from https://www.abs.gov.au

[3] Hunter Institute of Mental Health. (2017). *Stories matter: The role of storytelling in strengthening families and communities*. Newcastle: Hunter Institute.

References

ABS. (2019). *Family transitions and household formation.* Australian Bureau of Statistics. https://www.abs.gov.au

ABS. (2023). *Family characteristics and transitions.* Australian Bureau of Statistics.

ACCC. (2024). *Scamwatch: Annual scam statistics.* https://www.scamwatch.gov.au

AIHW. (2022). *Grandparent care in Australia.* Australian Institute of Health and Welfare.

AIHW. (2023). *Telehealth use during COVID-19 and beyond.* https://www.aihw.gov.au/reports/primary-health-care/telehealth-use

AIHW. (2024). *Telehealth activity statistics.* https://www.aihw.gov.au

Andrews, J. (2017, October 10). Julie Andrews on motherhood and independence. *The Guardian.* https://www.theguardian.com

Archer, M. (2019). Cultural scripts and family transitions: A cross-cultural analysis. *Journal of Family Studies, 25*(3), 289–305.

Australian Banking Association. (2023). *Bank branch closure trends in Australia.* https://www.ausbanking.org.au

Australian Cyber Security Centre. (2023). *Protect yourself online: Cybersecurity tips.* https://www.cyber.gov.au

Australian Housing and Urban Research Institute (AHURI). (2022). *Young adults, housing affordability and intergenerational living (Final Report No. 383).* https://www.ahuri.edu.au/research/final-reports/383

Australian Institute of Family Studies. (2022). *Grandparenting in contemporary Australia.*

Australian Institute of Family Studies (AIFS). (2025, February). *Divorces in Australia — Facts & figures* 2024.https://aifs.gov.au/research/facts-and-figures/divorces-australia-2024

Australian Seniors. (2024). *Empty nesters report 2024: Boomerang kids are returning to the nest, but empty nesters would prefer their space* [Research report]. https://www.seniors.com.au/documents/media-release-empty-nesters-report-2024.pdf

Australian Seniors. (2024). The Grandparent Report: Intergenerational bonds in modern Australia.

Bedford, O., & Yeh, K.-H. (2019). The history and the future of the psychology of filial piety: Chinese norms to contextualised personality construct. *Frontiers in Psychology*, 10, 100. https://doi.org/10.3389/fpsyg.2019.00100

Berndt, R. M., & Berndt, C. H. (1999). The world of the first Australians: Aboriginal traditional life, past and present(5th ed.). Aboriginal Studies Press.

Beyond Blue. (2021). The mental health of Australians in midlife: Stress, menopause, and life transitions. Beyond Blue Research Report.

Boss, P. (1999). Ambiguous loss: Learning to live with unresolved grief. Harvard University Press.

Boss, P. (2006). Loss, trauma, and resilience: Therapeutic work with ambiguous loss. W.W. Norton.

Change.org Australia. (2023). *About us.* https://www.change.org

Department of Employment and Workplace Relations. (2021). *Employment barriers for mature-age Australians research project.*

https://www.dewr.gov.au

de Botton, A. (2002). *The art of travel*. Hamish Hamilton.

Fiese, B. H., & Sameroff, A. J. (1999). Cultural scripts: How culture shapes family stories. *Family Process, 38*(4), 399–408.

Goleman, D. (1995). Emotional intelligence: Why it can matter more than IQ. Bantam Books.

Good Things Foundation Australia. (2024). *Be Connected program*. https://www.beconnected.esafety.gov.au

Jean Hailes for Women's Health. (2024/2025). *Menopause & sex (fact sheet hub)*.https://www.jeanhailes.org.au/resources/menopause-sex

Journal of Family Psychology. (2023). Grandparenthood and emotional well-being: A longitudinal study. *Journal of Family Psychology, 37*(4), 512–526.

Joseph, S. (1999). Intimate selving in Arab families: Gender, self, and identity. Syracuse University Press.

Kiecolt-Glaser, J. K., & Glaser, R. (2002). Depression and immune function: Central pathways to morbidity and mortality. *Journal of Psychosomatic Research*, 53(4), 873–876. https://doi.org/10.1016/S0022-3999(02)00309-4

Markus, A., & Kirpitchenko, L. (2021). Australia's multicultural families: Patterns of interdependence and independence. *Journal of Intercultural Studies*, 42(5), 601–618. https://doi.org/10.1080/07256868.2021.1977167

McCubbin, H. I., & Patterson, J. M. (1983). The family stress process: The Double ABCX model of adjustment and adaptation. In H. McCubbin et al. (Eds.), *Social stress and the family* (pp. 7–37). Routledge.

MyGov. (2024). *What you can do on myGov*. https://www.my.gov.au

NBN Co. (2024). *Regional rollout and connectivity updates.* https://www.nbnco.com.au

Newman, K. S. (2012). The accordion family: Boomerang kids, anxious parents, and the private toll of global competition. Beacon Press.

Novak, L. (2018, September 25). Research shows that parents still worry about grown children. *Do You Remember.*https://doyouremember.com/85108/parents-still-worry-about-grown-children

NSW Government. (2023). *Tech Savvy Seniors program.* https://www.sl.nsw.gov.au/public-library-services/learning/tech-savvy-seniors

Onyx, J., & Leonard, R. (2005). Australian grey nomads and "white settlers": New leisure lifestyles and retirement. *Annals of Leisure Research,* 8(1), 50–61. https://doi.org/10.1080/11745398.2005.10600941

Perel, E. (2017). The state of affairs: Rethinking infidelity. HarperCollins.

Psychiatric Association of Greece. (2019). Empty-nest-related psychosocial stress: Conceptual issues, future directions in economic crisis. *Psychiatriki,* 30(4), 329–338. https://www.psychiatriki-journal.gr/documents/psychiatry/30.4-EN-2019-329.pdf

Relationships Australia. (2023). *Empty nesters: Navigating life transitions.* https://www.relationships.org.au/empty-nesters/

Reserve Bank of Australia. (2023). *Trends in payments, banking, and digital adoption.* https://www.rba.gov.au

Rubin, R. (2017). When parents let go: The empty nest and identity shifts in mothers. *Journal of Women & Aging,* 29(3), 201–219. https://doi.org/10.1080/08952841.2016.1182114

Services Australia. (2024). *Digital service delivery and online access.* https://www.servicesaustralia.gov.au

Tracy, C., Putney, B., & Papp, L. M. (2021). A dyadic examination of marital quality at the empty-nest phase. *The Family Journal,* 29(4), 371–381. https://doi.org/10.1177/10664807211027287

Trautmann, S., & colleagues. (n.d.). Empty nest syndrome: Parents are happiest when their kids grow up. *Fatherly.* https://www.fatherly.com/health/empty-nest-syndrome-parents-happiest-when-kids-grow-up

Umberson, D., Pudrovska, T., & Reczek, C. (2010). Parenthood, childlessness, and well-being: A life course perspective. *Journal of Marriage and Family, 72*(3), 612–629. https://doi.org/10.1111/j.1741-3737.2010.00721.x

Wilson, E., & Harris, C. (2006). Meaningful travel: Women, independent travel and the search for self and meaning. *Tourism, 54*(2), 161–172. https://doi.org/10.1007/BF03216607

www.ingramcontent.com/pod-product-compliance
Lightning Source LLC
Chambersburg PA
CBHW030914090426
42737CB00007B/192